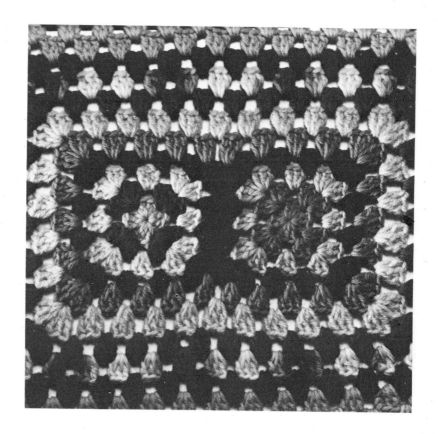

crochet

A Complete Introduction to the Craft of Crocheting

Emily Wildman

Conceived and edited by
William and Shirley Sayles

PAN BOOKS LTD : LONDON

Heirloom bedspread, 1935. Made in sections, then joined. Border was added after joining. 100% wool in shades of one colour

First British edition published 1973 by Pan Books Ltd,
33 Tothill Street, London SW1

ISBN 0 330 23785 3

2nd printing 1976

© 1972 by Western Publishing Company, Inc

Filmset and printed Offset Litho in Great Britain by
Cox & Wyman Ltd, London, Fakenham and Reading

Contents

ACKNOWLEDGEMENTS

Thanks are due to the Brooklyn Museum and to the
Metropolitan Museum of Art for permission to photograph
items from their collections; to the American Crafts Council,
and to the Canadian Guild of Crafts, Ontario, for their help
in providing photographs. Thanks go also to Mr and Mrs
Milton Fisher for so graciously allowing their home to be
used as background for many of the photographs shown in
this book.

Among those who have assisted in the preparation of this
book, special thanks are due to:

Louis Mervar, *Photography*
Dagfinn Olsen, *Diagrams*
Remo Cosentino, *Design and Production*

Also available in this series
POTTERY, FRAMING, MACRAMÉ, JEWELLERY,
RUGMAKING, CANDLEMAKING and WEAVING

Introduction

Crochet, a word familiar to practically everybody, is one of the most popular members of the needlecraft family. It is a simple technique that produces quick and satisfying results. It does not require a great deal of attention or concentration and yet, with it, you can make any item from fine lace tablecloths, doilies, and placemats to stoles, bedspreads and heavyweight rugs, or even constructions as varied in purpose and technique as the ones shown on these two pages.

THE STITCHES

All crochet begins with a slip knot and builds upon a base of chain stitches. One hand controls the tension of the wool; the other hand wields the crochet hook as it moves freely and swiftly to produce the fabric, pulling one loop through another loop in endless variations on the basic stitches. The first of the basic stitches, double crochet, is but one step beyond the chain stitch; all the others are based on double crochet, but with variations.

By combining two or more stitches, or by using one stitch in a variation, different pattern stitches are developed. Thus the repertoire and fascination of crochet continues to build, always based upon and using the same basic stitches.

THE HOOKS

The crochet hooks used to manipulate the stitch loops come in many different sizes and are composed of various materials. With fine crochet thread you would use a small steel hook (the finest of the hooks); with a heavier wool you would use a larger hook of aluminium or plastic; and with a very heavy wool, or one used in doubled strands, you would use a very large wooden hook.

The size of the crochet hook can have great influence on the appearance of any pattern, as can the weight and type of wool used. To see the difference for yourself, work up sample swatches using various-sized hooks and different weights of wool. By working these swatches you will quickly become aware that crochet, even though a simply worked technique, is also one of many possibilities.

A LOOK BACK

Even in 1858, some of the reasons for crochet's appeal were established when it was stated that '. . . crochet has now been for some years one of the most popular of all the various forms of fancy needle-work. The beauty and variety of the patterns that can be

This sturdy tote bag, crocheted of sisal twine, can also be used as a basket or plant holder

(Facing page) Circular three-dimensional crocheted forms. An example of the possibilities for crochet technique

Crocheted perfume case. Strawberry motifs in green and pink silk on a silver ground 5.4 cms×5.1 cms (2⅛″×2″). Handles and tassels attached

executed from it have perhaps been the chief cause of the great and universal preference manifested for crochet; but it owes, no doubt, also, something to its great durability, and to the facility with which a mistake can be remedied, without entangling or spoiling the work.'

The author of that quote summed up well the attributes of crochet even though the reference was to delicate crochet lace and not to the more sturdy, and even more durable, crochet so prevalent today. Fashions change, but crochet lace continues to attract interest. The older pieces, such as the ones shown on these pages, are in the treasured collections of museums in this country and abroad, and are sought after by fashion designers for study.

THE YARNS

Yarns come in a rich variety of natural and man-made fibres. Each has its own characteristics and may differ from another in texture, strength, weight, or tactile quality. Some may be too fuzzy for the purpose you have in mind. It is important, therefore, to know how they differ. Such knowledge will come in time and with experience.

(Facing page) Crocheted collar of the late 19th century. The tiny, evenly spaced motifs are made in very fine thread on a delicately worked ground

(Detail) Example of delicate crochet lace edging, c. 1880. A number of motifs are linked together in a repeat pattern

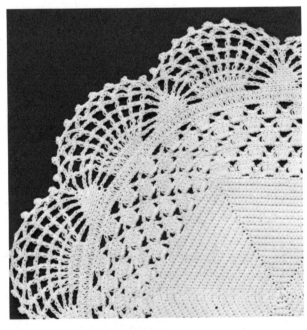

(Detail) Lace doily with three distinct patterns, c. 1875. The round piece is worked around a hexagonal centre. Picots edge the border scallops

A swatch is particularly valuable here for trying out yarns and will help you become familiar with them.

IN THIS BOOK

The basic stitches in this book are illustrated in clearly drawn diagrams for both the right-handed and the left-handed crocheter. The stitches are learned in no time at all by working them while following the instructions. There is also a variety of pattern stitches, motifs, and edgings. Still other patterns are used in the many projects given. On the last page is reference material and a list of suppliers.

Crochet instructions are written mostly in abbreviations. These are easily remembered, but there are tables on pages 12 and 19 to be referred to if you are in doubt. All the abbreviations are standard except for eon (each of next), which is original with this book and is used only on pages 56–9. *Work the instructions step by step; do not read ahead, since by doing so you may miss something of importance.*

(Below) 'Desert Flower', wall hanging, approx. 112 cms (44") square made of wool and mohair on velvet, 1971. Double and treble crochet stitches. Feathers adorn centre

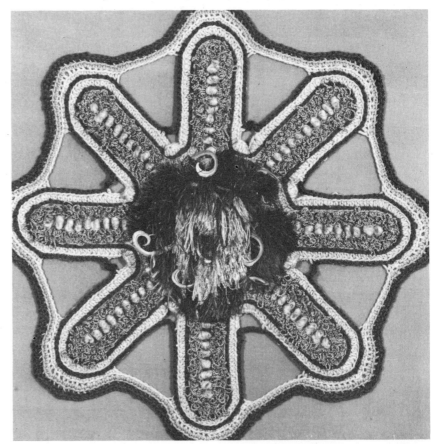

(Above) Crocheted headdress on a handcrafted form, 1971. The piece is crocheted of rug wool in chain stitch

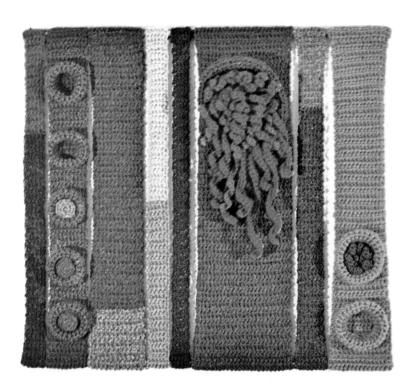

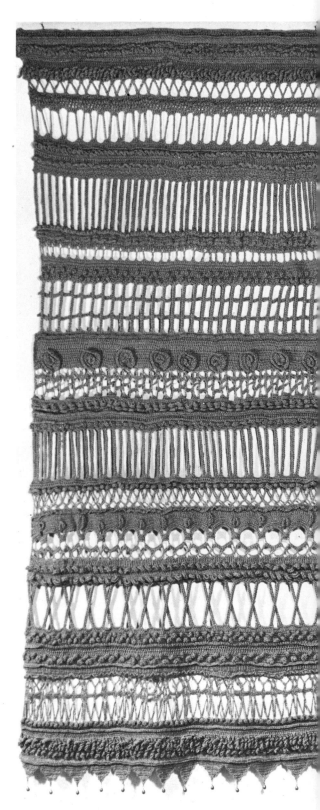

(Above) Crocheted wall hanging. Circular areas built up within some vertical colour bands add to textural interest

(Right) 'Victoria', detail of hanging or room divider, approx. 91 cms× 158 cms (36"×62"), made of natural jute string in double, treble and improvised crochet stitches

A LOOK AHEAD

Crochet is a healthy, viable craft. It was flourishing in the days when it was first discovered to be an easy substitute for lace-making. It was worked then with threads as fine as a human hair to produce various imitations of netting. It is flourishing today as a large contributor to our fashions. Seemingly, it will continue to flourish no matter what the time period. The range of its flexibility is even more evident now that it is being experimented with for still further interpretation. As testimony to its new development are the art forms shown on these pages. Further creative approaches are challenges to contemplate for the mind as well as the fingers, for there seems to be no limit to the potentials in the simple functional beauty of this technique.

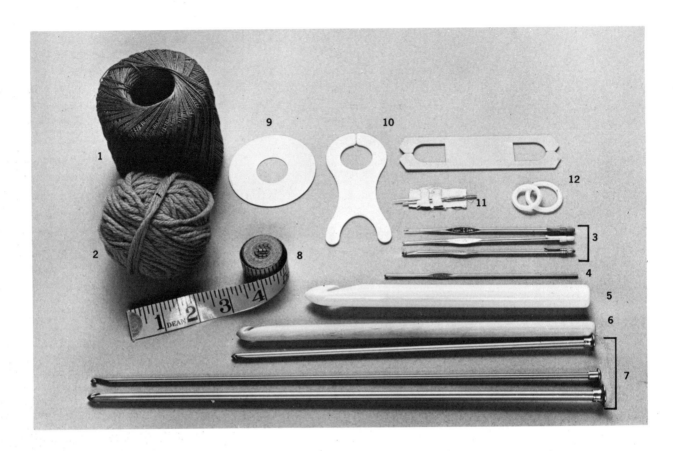

Equipment

A crochet hook and some yarn are all that are necessary to make a crocheted piece. The hooks and yarn pictured above are **1.** Cotton thread, **2.** Wool, **3.** Steel hooks, **4.** Aluminium hook, **5.** Plastic hook, **6.** Wooden hook, **7.** Tunisian hooks. The other items shown are **8.** Tape measure, **9.** Pompon circle, **10.** Bobbins, **11.** Tapestry needles, **12.** Plastic rings (for special projects).

Yarns for crochet are available in a wide variety of colours, weights, and textures (see yarn chart, facing page). Cotton comes in different weights from thin thread to heavy rug wool. Some cotton threads are mercerized for a lustrous finish (an example is pearl cotton). Linen comes 70/2 (finest) to $1\frac{1}{2}$ (heaviest). Wools and synthetics range widely from lightweight baby and fingering wools, light- to medium-weight Aran wool, chunky knitting wool through to heavy-weight rug wool. Still other materials that can be used include silk, ribbon, mohair, chenille, rattail rayon, metallic thread, string, sisal, raffia, flax, leather, and plastic lanyard. Although projects in this book call for specific materials, there are no rules limiting a fibre to a particular use; your choice is determined by the effect you wish to achieve.

Winding wool off revolving wool winder

Since different dye lots of a colour may vary, purchase enough wool at one time to finish your item. To estimate the amount of wool needed, either refer to a similar project or work a skein in the desired pattern and gauge, measure the result, and divide it into the total size.

The wrapper around each skein or ball of wool states wool type, skein weight, fibre content, colour, and dye lot number; sometimes included is whether wool is mothproof, colourfast, pre-shrunk or machine washable. However, it is always wise to test colourfastness and shrink resistance by crocheting a 15 cm (6″) square swatch and washing it before beginning your project.

Ball winding. Most wools are packaged in ready-to-use balls; others, in 'butterfly' skeins that must be wound in a ball. Wind loosely to avoid stretching the wool. Loop the skein around a chair back, a helper's hands, or a wool winder (facing page), cut the tie that holds the skein together, and start the ball by winding the wool over the fingers of one hand. After a number of turns, remove the wool, turn it parallel to the fingers, and resume winding around the fingers (and the wound wool). Continue in this fashion, changing direction occasionally.

Crochet hooks come in steel, aluminium, plastic and wood and are sized according to thickness. The finer the wool, the smaller the size hook used; the thicker the wool, the larger the size hook used. *Steel hooks*, the finest, are used mainly with fingering wool, thin linen, and cotton. They are numbered in reverse order from 0.60 (smallest) to 3.00 (largest). *Aluminium and plastic hooks*, used mainly with wool and synthetic wools and coarse cotton, are sized in increasing order from 1.25 (smallest) to 7.00 (largest). Manufacturers size these hooks by number. *Wooden hooks*, used mainly with heavy, bulky wool, come 10 (smallest), 13, 14, and 15 (largest). *Tunisian hooks*, used for the Tunisian stitch, look like knitting needles with a crochet hook at one end. They are aluminium, come in a variety of lengths, and are sized as crochet hooks. Special extending Tunisian hooks can be bought for making blankets (hook extends to 60 cms [24″]).

CROCHET HOOK SIZES

English	7.00	6.00	5.50	5.00	4.50	4.00	3.50	3.00	3.00	2.50
Continental	7	6	$5\frac{1}{2}$	5	$4\frac{1}{2}$	4	$3\frac{1}{2}$	$3\frac{1}{4}$	$3-2\frac{3}{4}$	$2\frac{1}{2}$

YARNS
1. Double knitting (wool)
2. Double knitting (orlon)
3. Crochet cotton
4. Rug wool
5. Rug wool (75% rayon, 25% cotton)
6. Rug wool (100% acrylic)
7. Chunky knitting wool
8. Pearl cotton/Carpet warp

NOVELTY YARNS
1. Lamé thread
2. Slub wool
3. Chenille
4. Rattail rayon No. 2
5. Cotton blend (67% cotton, 33% linen)

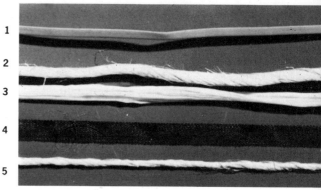

OTHER MATERIALS
1. Plastic lanyard
2. Sisal twine
3. Raffia
4. Ribbon
5. Flax

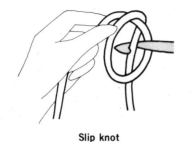

Slip knot

Holding the work. Note that hook is held in the same manner as a table-knife in cutting position

STARTING THE WORK RIGHT-HANDED

All crochet begins with a slip knot. Make a loop about 10 cms (4″) from wool end and hold between thumb and forefinger. Place wool strand behind loop and draw through as shown. Pull wool ends to tighten loop, but not so tight that hook cannot pass through freely.

Holding the work. You may find holding the work awkward at first, but ease will come with practice. The principle is to arrange the wool so that it feeds easily and at a regulated tension, and to hold the hook in a comfortable position. One way to arrange wool is to loop it around forefinger and hold it in place under last two fingers and against palm. Hold base of stitch between thumb and middle finger. Photo shows how to hold hook: as you would a knife in a cutting position – between thumb and forefinger and resting lightly on the other fingers. (Hook can also be held as you would a pencil, bringing middle finger forward to rest near tip.)

ABBREVIATED CROCHET TERMS

beg – beginning	**qd tr** – quadruple treble crochet
ch(s) – chain(s) or chain stitch	**rep(s)** – repeat(s)
cl – cluster	**rnd** – round
dble tr – double treble crochet	**sk** – skip
dc – double crochet	**sl st** – slip stitch
dec(s) – decrease(s)	**sp(s)** – space(s)
eon – each of next	**st(s)** – stitch(es)
htr – half treble crochet	**tog** – together
inc(s) – increase(s)	**tr** – treble crochet
lp(s) – loop(s)	**tr tr** – triple treble crochet
patt – pattern	**wrh** – wool round hook
pr r – previous row or round	

---

* – repeat instructions from asterisk as many more times as directed in addition to the original

× – times

( ) – work instructions in parentheses as many times as directed, for example: (2 dc into next tr)3× means to work stitches enclosed in parentheses 3 times in all

---

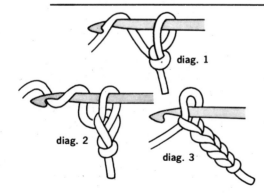

diag. 1

diag. 2

diag. 3

CHAIN STITCH (ch)

All crochet builds on a base of chain stitches.

1. Pass hook under wool and catch wool with hook **(diag. 1)**. This is called wool round hook (wrh).

2. Draw wool through loop on hook **(diag. 2)**. Do not work tightly. One chain stitch (ch) completed.

3. Continue wool round hook and draw through a new loop **(diag. 3)** for the number of chain stitches required. Keep thumb and forefinger near stitch (st) you are working on. This keeps chain from twisting.

> **Unless directions specify otherwise:** *Always* insert hook under the *two top* loops (strands) of a stitch. *Always* insert hook from *front* to *back*. There will *always* be one loop left on hook. *Do not work tightly.*
>
> Practise each stitch until you are familiar with it. Start your practice piece on a chain of 15 to 20 stitches, using double knitting wool and 6.50 hook.

DOUBLE CROCHET STITCH (dc)

Double crochet is the shortest of the basic stitches.

Make a chain of desired length.

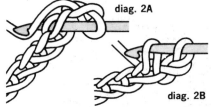

diag. 1

1. Insert hook under the two top loops in 2nd chain stitch (ch) from hook **(diag. 1)**.

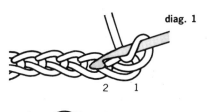

diag. 2A

diag. 2B

2. Wool round hook **(diag. 2A)** and draw wool through chain stitch. There are now 2 loops on hook **(diag. 2B)**.

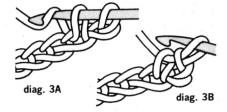

diag. 3A

diag. 3B

3. Wool round hook **(diag. 3A)** and draw it through the 2 loops on hook **(diag. 3B)**. This completes one double crochet (dc).

diag. 4

4. Insert hook into next chain stitch **(diag. 4)**. Repeat steps 2 and 3 and work a double crochet in each chain across.

diag. 5

5. At the end of row, chain 1 **(diag. 5)** and turn work so reverse side is facing you.

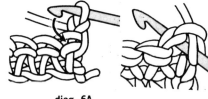

diag. 6A

diag. 6B

6. On following rows, insert hook in first stitch (st) of previous row **(diags. 6A, 6B)**. Repeat steps 2 and 3 and do double crochet in each st across. Chain (ch) 1 and turn.

TREBLE CROCHET STITCH (tr)

Treble crochet is twice as tall as double crochet. These two stitches are the ones most commonly used.

Make a chain of desired length.

diag. 1

1. Wool round hook (wrh) and insert hook into 4th chain stitch (ch) from hook **(diag. 1)**.

diag. 2

2. Wrh and draw wool through **(diag. 2)**. There are now 3 loops on hook.

diag. 3A

diag. 3B

3. Wrh **(diag. 3A)**, and draw wool through 2 loops. There are now 2 loops on hook **(diag. 3B)**.

diag. 4A

4. Wrh and draw wool through the 2 loops (lps) on hook **(diag. 4A)**. One treble crochet (tr) completed **(diag. 4B)**.

diag. 4B

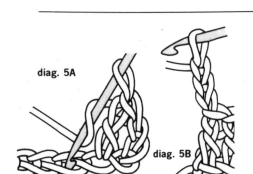

diag. 5A

5. Wrh and insert hook into next ch **(diag. 5A)**. Repeat (rep) steps 2–4 and make a tr in each ch across. At end of row, ch 3 **(diag. 5B)** and turn.

diag. 5B

6. On following rows, skip first st, wrh, and insert hook into 2nd st **(diag. 6)**. (The turning ch-3 at end of previous row counts as first tr of next row; therefore first tr of every row is always skipped.) Rep steps 2–4 and do tr in each st across.

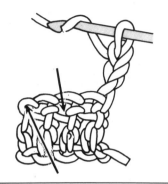

diag. 6

7. Work last tr of row in 3rd ch of turning ch-3 of previous row **(diag. 7)**. This keeps the work even. Ch 3 and turn.

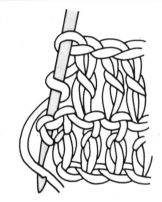

diag. 7

HALF TREBLE CROCHET STITCH (htr)

Taller than double crochet but not so tall as treble crochet.

Make a chain of desired length.

1. Wrh and insert hook into 3rd ch from hook **(diag. 1)**.

diag. 1

2. Wrh and draw wool through ch. There are now 3 loops (lps) on hook **(diag. 2A)**. Wrh and draw through the 3 lps on hook **(diag. 2B)**. One half treble crochet (htr) completed.

diag. 2A

3. Wrh, insert hook into next ch. Rep step 2 and do htr in each ch across. At end of row ch 2 and turn.

4. On following rows, wrh and insert hook in first st (in htr the turning ch does not count as first htr). Rep step 2 and do htr in each st across. Ch 2 and turn.

diag. 2B

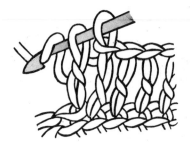

INCREASE (inc)

An increase is usually made by working two sts in the same st, but it may also be made, in any st but dc, by working a st in the very first st – the one usually skipped because of the turning chain.

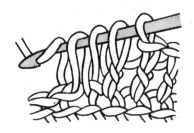

DECREASE (dec)

To decrease in double crochet: Insert hook into st, wrh and draw through a lp. Insert hook into next st, wrh and draw through a lp. Wrh and draw through the 3 lps on hook.

To decrease in double crochet: (wrh, insert hook into next st and draw through a lp, wrh and draw through 2 lps)2×. (3 lps on hook.) Wrh and draw through the remaining 3 lps.

To dec in other sts, just inc the number of lps on hook. A dec can also be made by skipping first st at beginning of row. Dec at end of row by skipping next to last st.

DOUBLE TREBLE CROCHET STITCH (dble tr)

Taller than double crochet, it produces looser work.

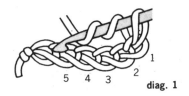

diag. 1

diag. 2A

diag. 2B

Make a chain of desired length.

1. Wrh twice and insert hook into 5th ch from hook (**diag. 1**).

2. Wrh, draw through a lp (4 lps on hook; **diag. 2A**), wrh, draw through 2 lps on hook (3 lps on hook, **diag. 2B**). Wrh and draw through 2 lps on hook 2 more times. One dble tr completed.

3. Wrh twice and insert hook into next ch (**diag. 3**). Rep step 2. Do a dble tr in each ch across. At end of row, ch 4, turn.

diag. 3

4. On following rows, insert hook into 2nd st (turning ch counts as first dble tr of next row). Work last dble tr of row in 4th ch of turning ch of previous row (**diag. 7**, page 15). Ch 4, turn.

TRIPLE TREBLE CROCHET STITCH (tr tr)

One stitch taller than double treble crochet, it is worked with an extra step, as follows: Wrh 3 times, insert hook into 6th ch from hook, wrh, draw through lp (5 lps on hook), wrh, draw through 2 lps at a time, 4 times. One tr tr completed (**diag. A**). Ch 5 to turn. Insert hook into 2nd st of next row.

QUADRUPLE TREBLE CROCHET (qd tr)

The tallest of the sts, it produces the loosest work. Wrh 4 times, insert hook into 7th ch and continue by working an extra step throughout (**diag. B**). Ch 6 to turn. Insert hook into 2nd st of next row.

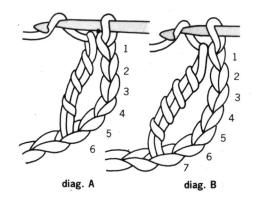

diag. A   diag. B

TO TURN WORK

Each stitch uses a different number of chain stitches to turn at the end of a row so as to bring the work into position for the next row. The length of the turning ch depends upon the length of the stitch that will be used to begin the row. Listed right for easy reference are the turning chs for the basic sts.

Double crochet (dc)	Ch 1 to turn
Half treble crochet (htr)	Ch 2 to turn
Treble crochet (tr)	Ch 3 to turn
Double treble crochet (dble tr) . .	Ch 4 to turn
Triple treble crochet (tr tr) . . .	Ch 5 to turn
Quadruple treble crochet (qd tr) .	Ch 6 to turn

SLIP STITCH (sl st) OR SINGLE CROCHET

A joining stitch used to form a chain into a ring, to join a round, or to join pieces invisibly. Also used to work across stitches for shaping or to strengthen edges. It adds no height to the work. When crochet directions say join, always do so with a sl st. A sl st is worked by inserting hook into a st, wrh (diag.) and drawing yarn through st and lp on hook in one motion.

To form a ring: Make a chain. Insert hook in first ch (**dia. A**), wrh, and pull through ch and loop on hook in one motion (**diag. B**).

To make a round (rnd): Make a ring. For the first round (each time around is called a 'round') work the stated number of stitches into ring (**diag. C**). Work next round into stitches of first round. Continue in this fashion, working each rnd into sts of previous rnd.

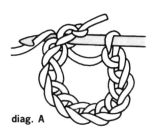

diag. A

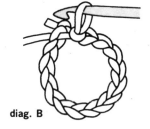

diag. B

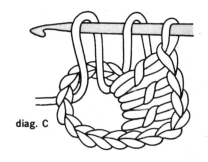

diag. C

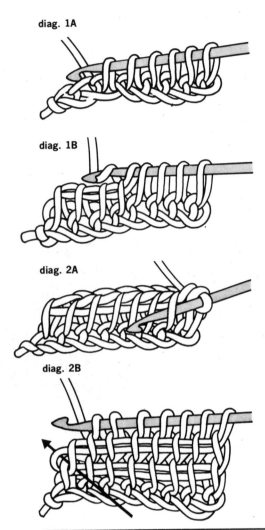

diag. 1A

diag. 1B

diag. 2A

diag. 2B

TUNISIAN STITCH SIMPLE

This stitch is completed in two rows (referred to as one row in instructions). In the first half, leave all loops on hook; in the second half, work loops off. *Do not turn work throughout.* Use a Tunisian hook.

Make a chain of desired length. *Note: On ch row only*, insert hook through *one* top loop instead of two.

Row 1:

A. Insert hook into top lp of 2nd ch from hook, wrh, draw through a lp. Rep in each ch across **(diag. 1A)**. *Leave all loops on hook.*

B. Work off loops. Wrh, draw through first lp on hook, * wrh and draw through 2 lps, rep from * across **(diag. 1B)**. The loop remaining on hook counts as first st of next row.

Row 2:

A. Keeping all lps on hook, insert hook under 2nd vertical bar **(diag. 2A)**, wrh, and draw through a lp. Rep for each bar across, ending insert hook under last bar and the st directly behind it, wrh and draw through a lp **(diag. 2B)**. This makes a firm edge.

B. Rep row 1B.

Rep row 2 for pattern. To finish, sl st in each bar across.

DECREASE FOR TUNISIAN STITCH SIMPLE

To dec one st, insert hook under the next 2 vertical bars, wrh, and draw through a loop (diag.).

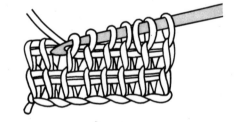

INCREASE FOR TUNISIAN STITCH SIMPLE

To inc one st, insert hook into ch between the next 2 vertical bars, wrh, and pull through a loop (diag.). Insert hook under next vertical bar, wrh and pull through a loop.

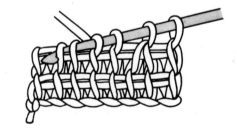

STARTING THE WORK LEFT-HANDED

All crochet begins with a slip knot. Make a loop about 10 cms (4″) from wool end and hold between thumb and forefinger. Place wool strand behind loop and draw through as shown. Pull wool ends to tighten loop, but not so tight that hook cannot pass through freely.

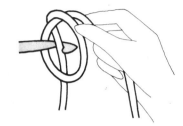

Slip Knot

Holding the work. You may find holding the work awkward at first, but ease will come with practice. The principle is to arrange the wool so that it feeds easily and at a regulated tension, and to hold the hook in a comfortable position. One way to arrange wool is to loop it around forefinger and hold it in place under last two fingers and against palm. Hold base of stitch between thumb and middle finger. Photo shows how to hold hook: as you would a knife in a cutting position – between thumb and forefinger and resting lightly on the other fingers. (Hook can also be held as you would a pencil, bringing middle finger forward to rest near tip.)

Holding the work. Note that hook is held in the same manner as a table-knife in cutting position

ABBREVIATED CROCHET TERMS

beg – beginning	**qd tr** – quadruple treble crochet
ch(s) – chain(s) or chain stitch	**rep(s)** – repeat(s)
cl – cluster	**rnd** – round
dble tr – double treble crochet	**sk** – skip
dc – double crochet	**sl st** – slip stitch
dec(s) – decrease(s)	**sp(s)** – space(s)
eon – each of next	**st(s)** – stitch(es)
htr – half treble crochet	**tog** – together
inc(s) – increase(s)	**tr** – treble crochet
lp(s) – loop(s)	**tr tr** – triple treble crochet
patt – pattern	**wrh** – wool round hook
pr r – previous row or round	

* – repeat instructions from asterisk as many more times as directed in addition to the original

× – times

( ) – work instructions in parentheses as many times as directed, for example: (2 dc into next tr)3× means to work stitches enclosed in parentheses 3 times in all

CHAIN STITCH (ch)

All crochet builds on a base of chain stitches.

1. Pass hook under wool and catch wool with hook **(diag. 1)**. This is called wool round hook (wrh).

2. Draw wool through loop on hook **(diag. 2)**. Do not work tightly. One chain stitch (ch) completed.

3. Continue to wool round hook and draw through a new loop **(diag. 3)** for the number of chain stitches required. Keep thumb and forefinger near stitch (st) you are working on. This keeps chain from twisting.

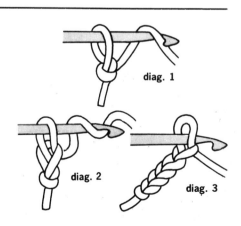

diag. 1

diag. 2

diag. 3

> **Unless directions specify otherwise:** *Always* insert hook under the *two top* loops (strands) of a stitch. *Always* insert hook from *front* to *back*. There will *always* be one loop left on hook. *Do not work tightly.*
>
> Practise each stitch until you are familiar with it. Start your practice piece on a chain of 15 to 20 stitches, using double knitting wool and a 6.50 hook.

diag. 1   1   2

DOUBLE CROCHET STITCH (dc)

Double crochet is the shortest of the basic stitches.

Make a chain of desired length.

diag. 2A   diag. 2B

1. Insert hook under the two top loops in 2nd chain stitch (ch) from hook **(diag. 1)**.

2. Wool round hook **(diag. 2A)** and draw wool through chain stitch. There are now 2 loops on hook **(diag. 2B)**.

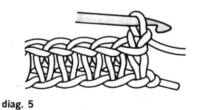

diag. 3A

diag. 3B

3. Wool round hook **(diag. 3A)** and draw it through the 2 loops on hook **(diag. 3B)**. This completes one double crochet (dc).

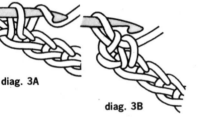

diag. 4

4. Insert hook into next chain stitch **(diag. 4)**. Repeat steps 2 and 3 and work a double crochet in each chain across.

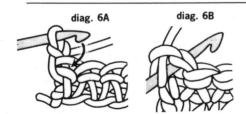

diag. 5

5. At end of row, chain 1 **(diag. 5)** and turn work so reverse side is facing you.

diag. 6A   diag. 6B

6. On following rows, insert hook in first stitch (st) of previous row **(diags. 6A, 6B)**. Repeat steps 2 and 3 and do double crochet in each st across. Chain (ch) 1 and turn.

TREBLE CROCHET STITCH (tr)

Treble crochet is twice as tall as double crochet. These two stitches are the ones most commonly used.

Make a chain of desired length.

1. Wool round hook (wrh) and insert hook into 4th chain stitch (ch) from hook **(diag. 1)**.

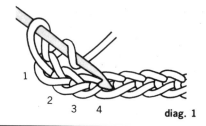

diag. 1

diag. 2

2. Wrh and draw wool through **(diag. 2)**. There are now 3 loops on hook.

3. Wrh **(diag. 3A)**, and draw wool through 2 loops. There are now 2 loops on hook **(diag. 3B)**.

diag. 3A

diag. 3B

4. Wrh and draw wool through the 2 loops (lps) on hook **(diag. 4A)**. One treble crochet (tr) completed **(diag. 4B)**.

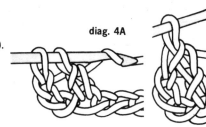

diag. 4B

diag. 4A

5. Wrh and insert hook into next ch **(diag. 5A)**. Repeat (rep) steps 2–4 and make a tr in each ch across. At end of row, ch 3 **(diag. 5B)** and turn.

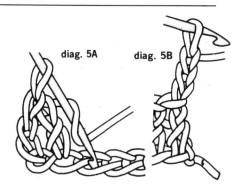

diag. 5A   diag. 5B

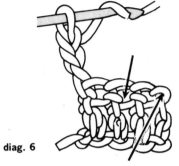

diag. 6

6. On following rows, skip first st, wrh, and insert hook into 2nd st **(diag. 6)**. (The turning ch-3 at end of previous row counts as first tr of next row; therefore first tr of every row is always skipped.) Rep steps 2–4 and do tr in each st across.

diag. 7

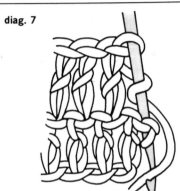

7. Work last tr of row in 3rd ch of turning ch-3 of previous row **(diag. 7)**. This keeps the work even. Ch 3 and turn.

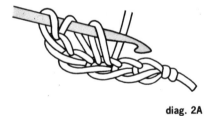

1   2   3   diag. 1

HALF TREBLE CROCHET STITCH (htr)

Taller than double crochet but not so tall as treble crochet.

Make a chain of desired length.

1. Wrh and insert hook into 3rd ch from hook **(diag. 1)**.

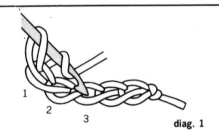

diag. 2A

2. Wrh and draw wool through ch. There are now 3 loops (lps) on hook **(diag. 2A)**. Wrh and draw through the 3 lps on hook **(diag. 2B)**. One half treble crochet (htr) completed.

diag. 2B

3. Wrh, insert hook into next ch. Rep step 2 and do htr in each ch across. At end of row ch 2 and turn.

4. On following rows, wrh and insert hook in first st (in htr, the turning ch does not count as first htr). Rep step 2 and do htr in each st across. Ch 2 and turn.

INCREASE (inc)

An increase is usually made by working two sts in the same st, but it may also be made, in any st but dc, by working a st in the very first st – the one usually skipped because of the turning chain.

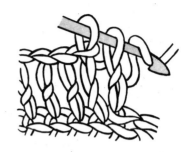

DECREASE (dec)

To decrease in double crochet: Insert hook into st, wrh and draw through a lp. Insert hook into next st, wrh and draw through a lp. Wrh and draw through the 3 lps on hook.

To decrease in treble crochet: (wrh, insert hook into next st and draw through a lp, wrh and draw through 2 lps)2×. (3 lps on hook.) Wrh and draw through the remaining 3 lps.

To dec in other sts, just inc the number of lps on hook. A dec can also be made by skipping first st at beginning of row. Dec at end of row by skipping next to last st.

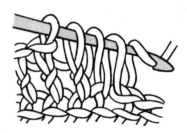

DOUBLE TREBLE STITCH (dble tr)

Taller than treble crochet, it produces looser work.

diag. 1

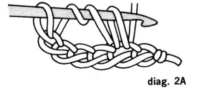

diag. 2A

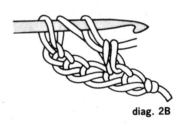

diag. 2B

Make a chain of desired length.

1. Wrh twice and insert hook into 5th ch from hook **(diag. 1)**.

2. Wrh, draw through a lp (4 lps on hook, **diag. 2A**), wrh, draw through 2 lps on hook (3 lps on hook, **diag. 2B**). Wrh and draw through 2 lps on hook 2 more times. One dble tr completed.

3. Wrh twice and insert hook into next ch **(diag. 3)**. Rep step 2. Do a dble tr in each ch across. At end of row, ch 4, turn.

4. On following rows, insert hook into 2nd st (turning ch counts as first dble tr of next row). Work last dble tr of row in 4th ch of turning ch of previous row **(diag. 7,** page 15). Ch 4, turn.

diag. 3

diag. A   diag. B

TRIPLE TREBLE CROCHET STITCH (tr tr)

One stitch taller than double treble crochet, it is worked with an extra step, as follows: Wrh 3 times, insert hook into 6th ch from hook, wrh, draw through lp (5 lps on hook), wrh, draw through 2 lps at a time, 4 times. One tr tr completed (**diag. A**). Ch 5 to turn. Insert hook into 2nd st of next row.

QUADRUPLE TREBLE CROCHET (qd tr)

The tallest of the sts, it produces the loosest work. Wrh 4 times, insert hook into 7th ch and continue by working an extra step throughout (**diag. B**). Ch 6 to turn. Insert hook into 2nd st of next row.

TO TURN WORK

Each stitch uses a different number of chain stitches to turn at the end of a row so as to bring the work into position for the next row. The length of the turning ch depends upon the length of the stitch that will be used to begin the row. Listed right for easy reference are the turning chs for the basic sts.

Double crochet (dc)	Ch 1 to turn
Half treble crochet (htr)	Ch 2 to turn
Treble crochet (tr)	Ch 3 to turn
Double treble crochet (dble tr) . .	Ch 4 to turn
Triple treble crochet (tr tr) . . .	Ch 5 to turn
Quadruple treble crochet (qd tr) .	Ch 6 to turn

SLIP STITCH (sl st) OR SINGLE STITCH

A joining stitch used to form a chain into a ring, to join a round, or to join pieces invisibly. Also used to work across stitches for shaping or to strengthen edges. It adds no height to the work. When crochet directions say join, always do so with a sl st. A sl st is worked by inserting hook into a st, wrh (diag.) and drawing wool through st and lp on hook in one motion.

To form a ring: Make a chain. Insert hook in first ch (**diag. A**), wrh, and pull through ch and loop on hook in one motion (**diag. B**).

To make a round (rnd): Make a ring. For the first round (each time around is called a 'round') work the stated number of stitches into ring (**diag. C**). Work next round into stitches of first round. Continue in this fashion, working each rnd into sts of previous rnd.

diag. A

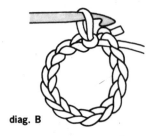

diag. B

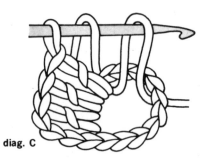

diag. C

TUNISIAN STITCH SIMPLE

This stitch is completed in two rows (referred to as one row in instructions). In the first half, leave all loops on hook; in the second half, work loops off. *Do not turn work throughout.* Use a Tunisian hook.

Make a chain of desired length. *Note: On ch row only,* insert hook through *one* top loop instead of two.

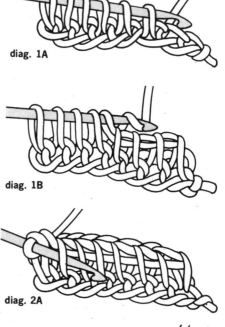

diag. 1A

diag. 1B

diag. 2A

Row 1:

A. Insert hook into top lp of 2nd ch from hook, wrh, draw through a lp. Rep in each ch across **(diag. 1A)**. *Leave all loops on hook.*

B. Work off loops. Wrh, draw through first lp on hook, * wrh and draw through 2 lps, rep from * across **(diag. 1B)**. The loop remaining on hook counts as first st of next row.

Row 2:

A. Keeping all lps on hook, insert hook under 2nd vertical bar **(diag. 2A)**, wrh, and draw through a lp. Rep for each bar across, ending insert hook under last bar and the st directly behind it, wrh and draw through a lp **(diag. 2B)**. This makes a firm edge.

B. Rep row 1B.

Rep row 2 for pattern. To finish, sl st in each bar across.

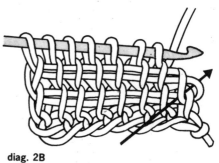

diag. 2B

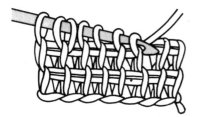

DECREASE FOR TUNISIAN STITCH SIMPLE

To dec one st, insert hook under the next 2 vertical bars, wrh, and draw through a loop (diag.).

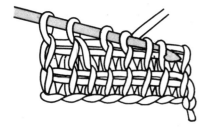

INCREASE FOR TUNISIAN STITCH SIMPLE

To inc one st, insert hook into ch between the next 2 vertical bars, wrh, and pull through a loop (diag.). Insert hook under next vertical bar, wrh and pull through a loop.

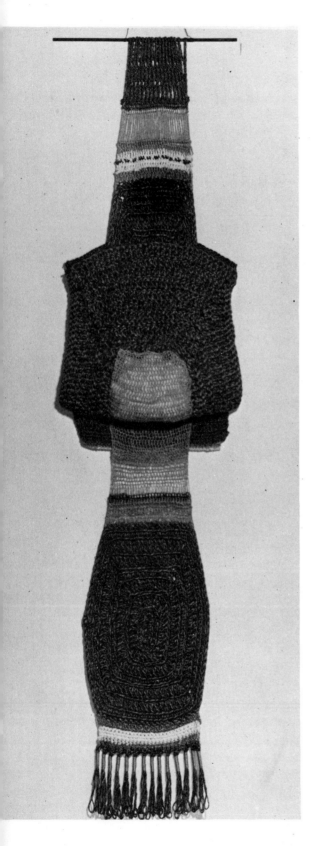

GAUGE

The gauge is the number of stitches and rows per centimetre. It determines the size of the item to be made and is always included in the directions. To check gauge, crochet and block a 10 cm (4″) square swatch, using stitch, wool, and hook specified. Place ruler on a row and count the number of stitches per cm; place ruler lengthways and count the number of rows per cm. If the measure is greater than the gauge, change to a larger hook – you are working too tightly; if it is less, change to a smaller hook – you are working too loosely. Hook size does not matter so long as gauge is correct.

MULTIPLES

Multiple of chain refers to the amount of chain stitches that must be made at the start of a piece if the pattern is to work out correctly. For example, if instructions call for a multiple of 10 ch, then chain 20, 30, 40, or any amount evenly divisible by 10. If multiple is $10+2$ ch, add 2 ch after the multiple is completed, for example, 22, 32, 42, etc.

Multiple of stitches refers to the number of sts in one pattern repeat. Should you wish to change to a different pattern in the course of your work, you would need to know its mult of sts. On page 80 is a list of multiples for pattern stitches and projects in this book.

BLOCKING

Blocking is used to shape a finished piece. Place piece on padded surface and pin sides, with heavy rustproof pins, while gently stretching to correct measurements. Place pins as close as necessary to obtain straight edges. Cover piece with a damp cloth and steam with an iron by supporting iron's weight in your hand and moving it above the piece *without touching it*. Remove pins when piece is thoroughly dry. If project is in sections, block each separately. Block raised or bulky patterns face up. Certain fibres do not require blocking, such as those sturdy enough to hold their shapes.

ENDING THE WORK

To fasten off, cut wool leaving an 8–10 cm (3–4″) tail and pull it through final loop. Weave in all tails at end of work. **To weave in**, thread each tail end with a tapestry needle and weave through areas of solid crochet to fasten securely. Trim remainder close to work.

'Circes Mandrake', approx. 51 cms × 1 m 70 cms (20″ × 65″). Wall hanging work in double and treble crochet with dyed hemp, linen, wool and string

JOINING

Sections are joined by slip stitching, sewing, or weaving them together. Use whatever method gives the best results. Join as invisibly as possible with matching wool (unless seam is part of design). Do not pull tightly – seams should have elasticity.

Slip stitching. Pin pieces, wrong sides facing. Insert hook into top loops of both pieces, catch wool, pull through, and knot over loops. Insert hook into same place, wrh, and draw through. Insert into next loops, wrh, and draw through loops on hook for first sl st. Continue along edges. Leave a 10 cm (4″) tail to be woven in.

Sewing. Pin pieces right sides facing. Insert threaded tapestry needle through top loops of both pieces, leaving a 10 cm (4″) tail. Secure stitch – do not knot. Sew close to edges.

Weaving. Lay pieces face up, edges meeting and follow diagram. Insert threaded tapestry needle in *centre* of loops throughout. If edges are uneven, sew rather than weave.

CHANGING COLOUR

When directions say to change colour, make stitch immediately preceding colour change *by working last wrh with 2nd colour*. Leave tail. When changing for a few stitches or over small areas, twist 1st colour around 2nd and carry it loosely across back until picked up again. Or 'work over' it. This means laying 1st colour across top of row being worked and working 2nd colour over it until needed. This method leaves fewer ends to weave in at the finish. It may also result in an uneven stitch; to compensate, work tighter. However, if the 1st colour is to be eliminated entirely, cut wool *(break off)* and fasten. Or lay it on top of previous row, work over it for a few stitches, then break off. When working with more than four colours, you may want to use bobbins to keep wool from tangling. Fill bobbins with colour changes and refill as needed.

ATTACHING NEW STRAND

Insert hook into stitch, loop new strand over hook and pull through. Remove hook, pull tail through and knot it to main strand. Insert hook into same place, catch wool, pull through, and continue work.

ATTACHING NEW THREAD

Attach new thread, preferably at the end of a row, leaving tails on both new and old threads. Do a regular stitch, working off last 2 loops with new thread. Work 3 or 4 rows to establish tension, then return to beginning and knot new thread to tail of old.

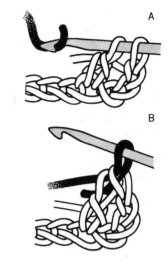

Changing colour by working last wrh stitch with second colour

Weaving: pull up needle in A, insert from *wrong* side in B, * insert from *right* side in next B loop, insert from wrong side in next A loop, insert from right side in next A loop, insert from wrong side in next B loop. Repeat from *

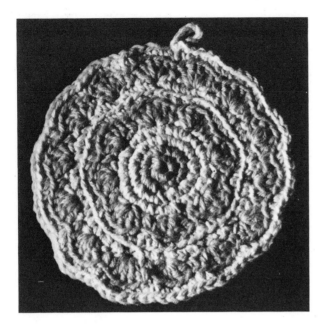

Texture in crochet is produced by the movement of the stitches; textural variation, by the way in which the stitches are combined in a pattern. On this and the following pages are patterns of different combinations – lace, cluster, raised and twisted (others can be found in projects throughout the book). *Note:* When practising patterns, make starting chain long enough to accommodate at least 3 pattern repeats.

shell

A group of 3 or more stitches worked in one stitch.

Multiple of 6+1 ch.

Row 1: 2 tr in 4th ch from hook (half shell made), * sk 2 ch, dc in next ch, sk 2 ch, 5 tr in next ch (shell made – see diag.). Rep from *, ending sk 2 ch, dc in last ch. Ch 3, turn.

Row 2: 2 tr in first dc of pr r, * dc in 3rd tr of shell, 5 tr in next dc. Rep from *, ending dc in top of turning ch-3. Ch 3, turn.

Rep row 2 for pattern.

filet mesh (or rug stitch)

An openwork pattern with many design variations.

Chain an even number.

Row 1: Tr in 4th ch from hook, * ch 1, sk 1 ch, tr in next ch, rep from * across. Ch 1, turn.

Row 2: Dc in first st, * dc in next ch-1 sp, dc in next tr, rep from * across. Ch 4, turn.

Row 3: Tr in 3rd st, * ch 1, sk 1 st, tr in next st, rep from * across. Ch 1, turn.

Rep rows 2 and 3 for pattern, ending with row 2.

open shell

A lacy variation of the basic shell.

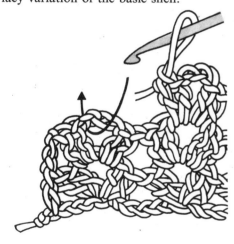

Multiple of 6+4 ch.

Row 1: Work (2 tr, ch 3, 2 tr) in 6th ch from hook (open shell made), * sk next 5 ch (2 tr, ch 3, 2 tr) in next ch. Rep from * across, ending sk 3 ch, tr in last ch. Ch 3, turn.

Row 2: * (2 tr, ch 3, 2 tr) in next ch-3 sp (see diag.). Rep from * across, ending tr in top of turning ch-3. Ch 3, turn.

Rep row 2 for pattern.

cluster

Two or more stitches gathered into a group.

Multiple of 3+1 ch.

Row 1: In 4th ch from hook work (wrh and draw through a lp, wrh and through 2 lps) twice, wrh and through the 3 lps on hook (beg cluster made), * ch 2, sk 2 ch, (wrh, insert hook in next ch, wrh, draw through a lp, wrh and through 2 lps)3×, wrh and through the 4 lps on hook – see diag. (cluster made). Rep from * across. Ch. 3, turn.

Row 2: (Wrh, insert hook in top of cl of pr r, draw through a lp, wrh and through 2 lps) twice, wrh and through the 3 lps on hook, * ch 2, make a cl in next cl of pr r. Rep from * across. Ch 3, turn.

Rep row 2 for pattern.

puff or hazelnut

A cluster stitch variation in a closed pattern.

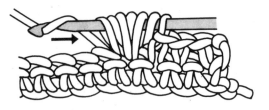

Multiple of 4 ch.

Row 1: (right side) Dc in 2nd ch from hook, * dc in next ch. Rep from * across. Ch 1, turn.

Row 2: Dc in first 3 sts, * wrh, insert hook into next st, wrh, draw through a lp (wrh, insert into same st, wrh, draw through a lp)2×, wrh and through the 7 lps on hook (diag.). One hazelnut st made. Dc in each of next 3 dc, rep from * across. Ch 1, turn.

Row 3: Dc in each st across, ch 1, turn.

Row 4: Dc in first st, * hazelnut st in next st, dc in each of next 3 sts. Rep from * across. Ch 1, turn.

Row 5: Dc in each st across. Ch 1, turn.

Rep rows 2–5 for pattern.

popcorn

This stitch gathers a shell into a fat cluster.

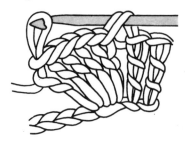

Multiple of 4+1 ch.

Row 1: (right side) Tr in 4th ch from hook, ch 1, 5 tr in next ch, remove hook from lp, insert hook, *front to back*, in top of first tr of 5-tr group, draw dropped lp through first tr (diag.), ch 1 to tighten (popcorn made), * tr in each of next 3 ch, popcorn in next ch. Rep from * across. Ch 3, turn.

Row 2: Tr in 2nd st (turning ch-3 counts as first tr), tr in next st, * ch 1, 5 tr in top of next popcorn of pr r, remove hook from lp, insert hook, *back to front*, in first tr of 5-tr group, draw dropped lp through first tr, ch 1 to tighten (popcorn made on right side), tr in each of next 3 tr. Rep from * across. Ch 3, turn.

Row 3: Rep row 2, except insert hook *front to back* for popcorn.

Rep rows 2 and 3 for pattern.

crossed treble crochet

A stitch with a twist in an alternating pattern.

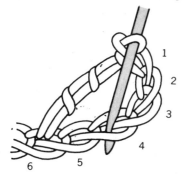

Chain an even number.

Row 1: Tr in 6th ch from hook (the first 3 chs count as first tr), ch 1; crossing over tr just made, tr in 4th ch from beg (diag.), * sk 2 ch, tr in next ch, ch 1; crossing over tr just made, tr in first ch of sk-2 ch. Rep from *, ending tr in last ch. Ch 4, turn.

Row 2: Sk first 2 tr, tr in next tr, ch 1, tr in last skipped tr, * sk tr, ch 1, tr in next tr, ch 1, tr in skipped tr. Rep from *, ending tr in 3rd ch of turning ch-4.

Rep row 2 for pattern.

solomon's knot

An open, long stitch, resembling netting.

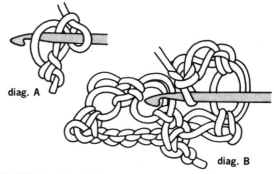

diag. A

diag. B

Multiple of 5+2 ch.

Row 1: Dc in 2nd ch from hook, * pull up lp on hook until it is 19.05 mms ($\frac{3}{4}''$) long, wrh, draw through a lp (making a long ch st), insert hook between lp and single strand of ch **(diag. A)** and work dc (single knot st made). Rep from * once more (double knot st made), sk next 4 ch, dc in next ch (knot completed). Rep from first * across, ending with 1 double and 2 single knot sts.

Row 2: * Dc in long lp of first knot st of pr r **(diag. B)**, dc in long lp of 2nd knot st, work a double knot st. Rep from * across, ending with 1 double and 2 single knot sts.

Rep row 2 for pattern.

GRANNY SQUARE

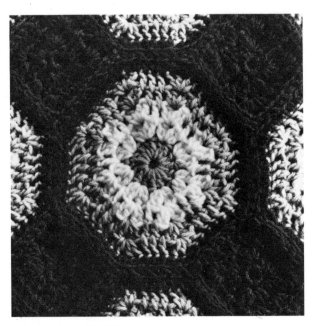

OCTAGON SWIRL

Motifs

Each symmetrically designed motif is a complete unit in itself, yet becomes a related part of the whole when joined with other motifs to form finished pieces. Motifs can also be used individually as decorative additions. *Note:* Do not turn. Always work with right side facing you.

granny square
Worked with four colours: A, B, C, D.

With A, ch 6, join with sl st to form ring (page 17 or 24).

Rnd 1: Ch 3, work 2 tr in ring, ch 2, work (3 tr in ring, ch 2)3×. Join with sl st to top of ch-3. Fasten off.

Rnd 2: Attach B in any ch-2 sp, ch 3, (2 tr, ch 2, 3 tr) in same ch-2 sp, ch 1, * (3 tr, ch 2, 3 tr) in next ch-2 sp, ch 1, rep from * twice more. Join with sl st to top of ch-3. Fasten off.

Rnd 3: Attach C in àny ch-2 sp, ch 3, (2 tr, ch 2, 3 tr) in same ch-2 sp, ch 1, 3 tr in next ch-1 sp, ch 1, * (3 tr, ch 2, 3 tr) in next ch-2 sp, ch 1, 3 tr in next ch-1 sp, ch 1, rep from * twice more. Join with sl st to top of ch-3. Fasten off.

Rnd 4: Attach D in any ch-2 sp, ch 3, (2 tr, ch 2, 3 tr) in same ch-2 sp, ch 1, (3 tr in next ch-1 sp, ch 1)2×, * (3 tr, ch 2, 3 tr) in next ch-2 sp, ch 1, (3 tr in next ch-1 sp, ch 1)2×, rep from * twice more. Join with sl st to top of ch-3. Fasten off.

octagon swirl
Worked with four colours: A, B, C, D.

With A, ch 6, join with sl st to form ring.

Rnd 1: Ch 3, work 15 tr in ring. Join with sl st to top of ch-3. Break off.

Rnd 2: Attach B to any st, (ch 3, 1 tr, ch 1, 2 tr) in same st, sk 1 st, * (2 tr, ch 1, 2 tr) in next st, sk 1 st, rep from * 6 more times (8 groups). Join to top of ch-3.

Rnd 3: Sl st across first tr to ch-1 sp, (ch 3, 1 tr, ch 1, 2 tr) in same sp, tr in sk-1 sp of pr r, * (2 tr, ch 1, 2 tr) in next ch-1 sp, tr in next sk-1 sp, rep from * 7 more times. Join to top of ch-3. Break off.

Rnd 4: Attach C to any ch-1 sp, (ch 3, 1 tr, ch 1, 2 tr) in same sp, sk 2 sts, 1 tr in each of next 2 sps, * (2 tr, ch 1, 2 tr) in next ch-1 sp, tr in each of next 2 sps (before and after tr of pr r), rep from * around. Join to top of ch-3.

Rnd 5: Sl st across first tr to ch-1 sp, (ch 3, 1 tr, ch 1, 2 tr) in same ch-1 sp, sk 2 sts, 1 tr in each of next 3

CIRCLE IN SQUARE

sps, * (2 tr, ch 1, 2 tr) in next ch-1 sp, sk 2 sts, 1 tr in each of next 3 sps, rep from * around. Join to top of ch-3. Break off.

Rnd 6: Attach D to any st, ch 1, work 1 htr in each st around and 2 htr in each ch-1 sp. Join to first st. Fasten off.

circle in square

Ch 8, join with sl st to form ring.

Rnd 1: Ch 5 (counts as first tr and ch 2), * 1 tr in ring, ch 2, rep from * 10 more times, ending sl st in 3rd ch of ch-5 (12 tr).

Rnd 2: Ch 3, tr in *back* loop of each st and ch around, ending sl st in top of ch-3 (36 tr).

Rnd 3: Ch 7 (counts as first tr and ch 4), sk 2 sts, * tr in *back* loop of next st, ch 4, sk 2 sts, rep from * around, ending sl st in 3rd ch of ch-7 (12 tr).

Rnd 4: Sl st in ch-4 sp of pr r, ch 4 (counts as first tr), 4 dble tr in same sp, ch 1, * 5 dble tr in next ch-4 sp, ch 1, rep from * around, ending sl st in 4th ch of ch-4 (60 dble tr).

Rnd 5: Ch 11 (counts as first dble tr and ch 7), sk 5 dble tr, * 1 dble tr in next ch-1 sp, ch 7, sk 5 dble tr, rep from * around, ending sl st in 4th ch of ch-11 (12 dble tr).

Rnd 6: Ch 1, dc in *back* loop of every st and ch around, ending sl st in first st (96 dc).

Rnd 7: * Ch 7, sk 7 sts, htr in next st, ch 1, tr in next st, ch 1, dble tr in next st, ch 7, sk 3 sts, dble tr in next st, ch 1, tr in next st, ch 1, htr in next st, ch 7, sk 7 sts, dc in next st, rep from * around (4 corners formed). End sl st in first ch. Fasten off.

working geometric shapes

By following the instructions given here, you will be able to make any geometric shape. Variations on some of these basic methods will be found in the motifs above and in projects throughout the book.

Square. Begin with a ring and work in a multiple of 4 sts, including incs. Shape square by dividing work into fourths, so that, for example, a rnd of 12 sts would divide into 4 groups of 3 sts each. You would then * work 1 st in each of next 2 sts, 3 sts into 3rd st (corner made), rep from * around. Join with sl st to beg st. Continue working evenly and putting 3 sts into one st at every corner.

A *hexagon* is worked in a multiple of 6 sts. Shape by dividing work into sixths and putting 3 sts into every 6th st. An *octagon* is worked in a multiple of 8 sts.

Oval. Make a ch (its length will be the difference between length and width of planned piece; for example, a 10 cm × 15 cm (4″ × 6″) piece would start on a 5 cm (2″) ch). Work one st in each ch across, ending with 3 sts in last ch. Do not turn work, but continue along bottom edge of ch, in top loop *only*, ending with 2 sts in last ch. Join with sl st to first st. Continue working, as in a round; inc by 3 sts at each end. As oval grows in size, inc further on curves to keep the work flat. Ch when needed.

Diamond, Triangle. Making diamonds and making triangles are really exercises in inc and dec. *For diamond:* ch 2 and work 2 sts in 2nd ch from hook, ch 1, turn. For next row work 2 sts in each of the 2 sts, ch 1, turn. Inc in first and last st of each row for desired width, then dec in first and last st of every row. Continue in this manner. *For triangle:* Work one half of diamond as above. Or start on a long ch and dec until only 2 or 3 sts remain.

Finishings

After your work is completed you may want to consider the following finishing touches – all of which are simple to do. The picots and reverse dc are trims to outline the work; they are crocheted into the edge of the finished piece. The small designs of the picots make them also suitable as insertions. The double ch, made separately and then sewn on, is used as cording, as a substitute for braids, or as a belt tie. It also provides a strong foundation to build work onto. Fringes, tassels, and pompons are versatile decorations that can be attached singly or in profusion. Finishings are sometimes worked in different wool weights and colour for emphasis.

Simple Picot

SIMPLE PICOT

Attach wool. With right side facing, sl st in first 2 sts, * dc in next st, ch 3, dc in same st as first dc, sl st in next 2 sts, rep from *.

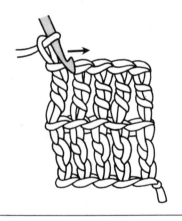

Picot

PICOT

Attach wool. With right side facing, dc in first st, * ch 5, sl st in 4th ch from hook, ch 1, sk next st, dc in next st, rep from *.

REVERSE DC

Attach wool. Work 1 row dc, ch 1, *but do not turn*, insert hook from front into first st to right of hook (diag.) and work a dc, * dc in next st to right of st just made, rep from *.

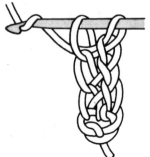

DOUBLE CH

Ch 2, dc in 2nd ch from hook, * insert hook under single top strand at *left* edge of last dc made (diag.), wrh and draw through a loop (2 loops on hook), wrh and through the 2 loops on hook, rep from * for desired length.

FRINGE

Wind wool around cardboard cut 2.5 cms (1″) longer than desired length of fringe (extra inch is for knot takeup) and cut along one edge. Insert hook into fabric, pick up the doubled strands of one group and pull through, forming a loop. Pull ends through loop, knotting them. Another row of knots can be added by knotting the halves of adjacent groups together.

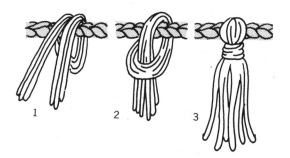

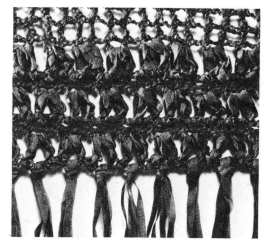

A four-strand ribbon fringe drawn through crocheted edge

TASSEL

Wind wool around cardboard cut to desired length of tassel. The number of times wool is wound around depends on how plump you wish to make tassel. Insert an extra length of wool through one end of group and tie securely. This length will be used to tie tassel to fabric. Cut strands at other end. Tightly wrap a second strand a few times around group 1.35–2.5 cms (½″ to 1″) below first, and knot it. Tie tassel around edge loop, sew down, and trim ends.

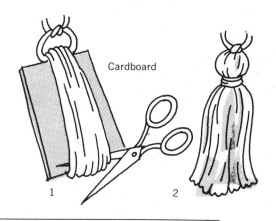

POMPON

Cut cardboard circles to desired size of pompon and cut a hole about 0.5 cm (¼″) in centre of each – or purchase plastic circles (they come in various sizes). Cut 4 lengths of wool, each 2.5 metres (3 yds) long. Place circles together and wind wool around, drawing it through centre and over edges. Continue until circles are completely covered and opening is filled in. Cut wool along outside edges. Slip a length of wool between the cardboards and wind it around very tightly several times; secure with a knot, leaving ends long enough to fasten pompon to fabric. Tear cardboards away. Fluff pompon and trim.

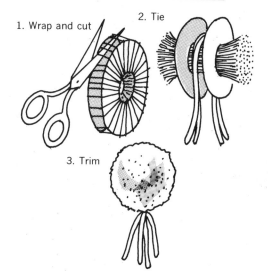

Tote Bags

The special feature of the tote bags shown on the facing page and on page 38 is the attractive use of unusual materials – sisal twine and plastic lanyard. Such materials produce sturdy, practical items that are relatively care free. The sisal tote is made in rounds: its base in double crochet, its sides in filet mesh. It can also be used as a decorative basket or a plant holder. The lanyard tote is worked with the open V stitch and is made in two sections that are later joined.

sisal tote bag or plant holder   28 cms (11″) deep, 28 cms diameter

Materials: Sisal twine, approx. 0.75 cm diameter, 180 metres (600 ft) or approx. 1 kilogramme (32 oz).
6.50 crochet hook.

Gauge: 2 dc = 2.5 cms (1″); 4 rows = 7.5 cms (3″).

PATTERN STITCH: Dc and filet mesh in rounds.

Ch 4, join with sl st to form ring.

Rnd 1: Ch 1, work 8 dc in ring. Join with sl st to first st.

Rnd 2: Ch 1, work 2 dc in each st around (16 sts). Join with sl st to first st.

Rnd 3: Ch 1, * 2 dc in next st, dc in next st, rep from * around (24 sts). Join with sl st to first st.

Rnd 4: Ch 1, * dc in each of next 2 sts, 2 dc in next st, rep from * around (32 sts). Join with sl st to first st.

Rnd 5: Ch 1, * 2 dc in next st, dc in each of next 3 sts, rep from * around (40 sts). Join.

Rnds 6–9: Continue to inc 8 sts evenly around for 4 more rounds (72 sts). For example: row 6 is worked, dc in each of next 4 sts, 2 dc in next st. Try not to put incs directly above each other. Base of tote bag or planter completed.

Rnds 10 & 11: Ch 1, work dc in each st around. Join.

Rnd 12: (Filet mesh) Ch 4, * sk 1 st, tr in next st, ch 1, rep from * around. Join with sl st to 3rd ch of ch-4.

Rnd 13: Ch 1, dc in st just joined, * dc in next ch-1 sp of pr r, dc in next tr, rep from * around. Join with sl st to first st.

Rep rows 12 and 13 until piece is 28 cms (11″) high, ending with row 13.

Fasten off, weave in ends. For tote bag, insert a handle – either crocheted or purchased – through filet mesh spaces. A nylon nautical rope, 1.35 cms (½″) in diameter was used here.

Base of sisal tote worked in rounds of double crochet

Detail of filet mesh stitches worked on sides of sisal tote

Tote bag, 28 cms (11″) deep, 28 cms diameter, made with sisal twine. Shown right with thick nylon rope handle and below as plant holder

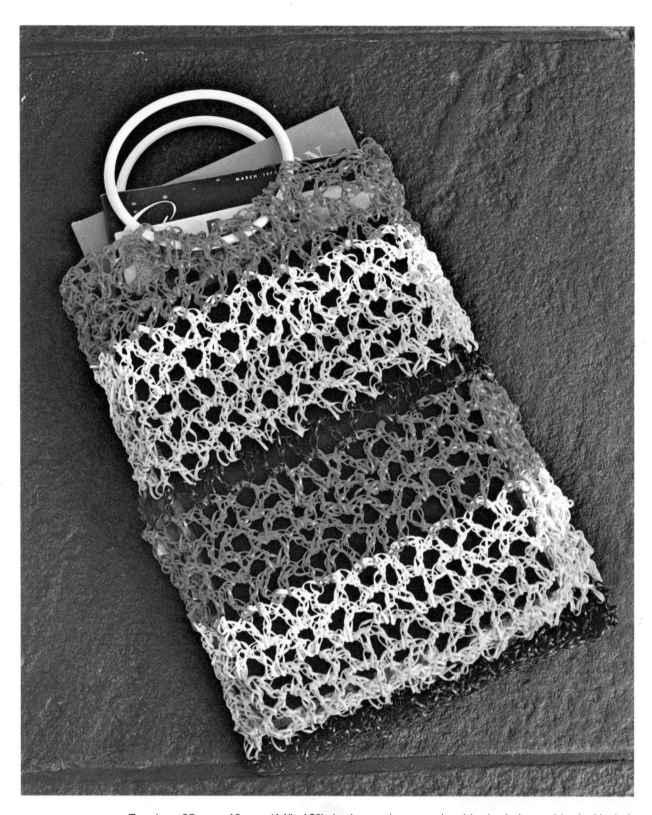

Tote bag, 35 cms×46 cms (14″×18″), in three colours, made with plastic lanyard in the V stitch

lanyard tote bag 35 cms × 46 cms (14″ × 18″)

Materials: Vinyl corded lace.
6.50 crochet hook. Circular handbag handles.
90 metres (100 yds) orange   45 metres (50 yds) white
70 metres (75 yds) yellow   23 metres (25 yds) green

Gauge: 1 V st = 2.5 cms (1″); 1 row = 2.5 cms (1″).

PATTERN STITCH: V stitch. Multiple of 3+6 ch.

First side: With green, ch 39.

Row 1: Tr in 6th ch from hook, * sk 2 ch, (tr, ch 2, tr) in next ch (V st made), rep from * across. Work last wrh and draw through 2 lps with yellow. (*Note:* All colour changes are done in this manner – working last wrh and drawing through new colour.) Break off green. With yellow, ch 5, turn.

Row 2: Tr in first ch-2 sp, * (tr, ch 2, tr) in next ch-2 sp, rep from * across, ending (tr, ch 2, tr) in lp of ch-5. Ch 5, turn.

Rep row 2 for pattern and change colours as follows:

3 rows yellow	3 rows yellow
2 rows white	2 rows white
4 rows orange	4 rows orange
1 row green	

Fasten off. Rep for second side. To finish: Weave sides tog. Sl st tog at bottom. Weave in ends. Place handles at top centre of each half, fold each top of tote bag over a handle, and sew in place.

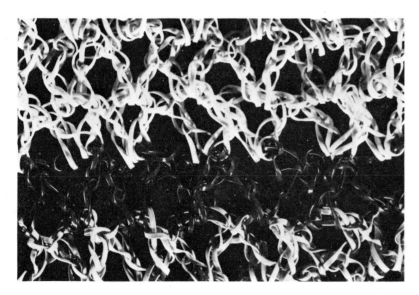

Detail of V stitch. Shown in the three colours used

Stoles and Shawl

Two stoles and one shawl – light, soft, and lacy but different texturally because of the stitches used. The pink stole (pictured on page 43) uses the Tunisian stitch with cluster, a combination that creates a circular effect in the design. The white shawl (facing page), made of fluffy mohair, is in the single knot stitch (the first half of Solomon's knot) and results in a delicate looped lace. The yellow stole (pictured on page 43) is made in double crochet pulled long and worked over a cardboard strip for a linear pattern. As with all projects in this book, change colours to suit your needs.

Detail of pink stole showing clusters formed in Tunisian stitch rows

pink stole 46 cms × 173 cms (18″ × 68″) (excluding fringe)

Materials: Chunky wool, fourteen 25 gm balls (12 oz).
6.50 Tunisian hook.

Gauge: 1 cluster = 2.5 cms (1″).

PATTERN STITCH: Lace Tunisian st with cluster (cl). Multiple of 4+1 ch. *Note:* Each Tunisian row is worked in 2 steps (page 18 or 25). *Do not turn work throughout.*

Ch 89 loosely.

Row 1:

A. *Keeping all loops on hook*, pick up a lp in top lp *only* of 2nd ch from hook and in each ch across (89 lps).

B. *Working loops off hook*, * ch 3, wrh and draw through 5 lps on hook (cl made), wrh and draw through one lp to tighten cl, rep from * across. One lp remains on hook. At end of row, ch 1.

Row 2:

A. Pick up a lp in top of each cl and in top lp of each ch of ch-3 across.
B. Same as row 1B.

Rep row 2 until piece measures 173 cms (68″), ending sl st in top of each cl and in top lp of each ch of ch-3 across. Fasten off.

To finish: With right side facing, attach wool to starting ch and sl st in each ch across. Weave in ends. Block. Make a 13 cm (5″) fringe; attach 4 doubled strands in every 4th sl st across each end of stole.

mohair shawl   168 cms × 84 cms (66″ × 33″) (excluding fringe)

Materials: Mohair wool, six 50 gm balls (9 oz).
4.00 crochet hook.

Gauge: 4 knots sts = 7.5 cms (3″); 7 rows = 7.5 cms (3″).

PATTERN STITCH: Single knot st. Chain is an even number.

Ch 150 loosely.

Row 1: Dc in 2nd ch from hook, * pull up lp on hook until it is 1.25 cms ($\frac{1}{2}$″) long, wrh and draw through a lp (long ch st made), insert hook between lp and single strand of ch (**diag. A,** page 31), and work 1 dc (single knot st made), sk 1 ch, dc in next ch, rep from * across. Ch 1, turn.

Row 2: Dc in long lp of first knot st of pr r (knot st dec made), * make a knot st, dc in next long lp st of pr r, rep from * across. Ch 1, turn.

Rep row 2 until 6 knot sts remain. Fasten off, weave in ends. To finish, attach wool to starting ch, work dc across. Fasten off. Make a 15 cm (6″) fringe; attach 4 doubled strands in each knot st around all edges but top edge.

VARIATION: If you want a rectangular-shaped shawl, rather than a triangular one, ch more sts on to start, work row 1, and change pattern row 2 as follows:

Dc in first dc of pr r, * make a knot st, dc in next long loop of pr r, rep from * across. Ch 1, turn.

White shawl made with mohair in the single knot stitch

Detail of white shawl showing single knot stitch (first half of Solomon's knot)

yellow stole 56 cms × 183 cms (22″ × 72″)

Materials: Chunky knitting wool. Seven 50 gm balls (12 oz).
6.50 crochet hook.
2 cardboard strips, 4 cms (1½″) and 7.5 cms (3″) wide; any length.

Gauge: 5 dc = 5 cms (2″).

PATTERN STITCH: Long dc. Chain is an even number.

Ch 180 loosely.

Row 1: Dc in 2nd ch from hook and in each ch across. Ch 1, turn.

Row 2: (Long dc) Pull up lp on hook to height of 4 cm (1½″) cardboard strip, place strip in front of lp. Working over strip, insert hook in first st, wrh, pull up lp to top of strip, wrh and through 2 lps on hook (long dc made), ch 1, sk next st, * long dc in next st, ch 1, sk next st, rep from * across. Ch 1, turn. Slide strip out of lps.

Row 3: Dc in first ch, dc in long dc, * dc in next ch, dc in next long dc, rep from * across. Ch 1, turn.

Row 4: Dc in each dc across.

Rep rows 2 and 3 for pattern, working row 2 once more with 4 cm (1½″) strip, then 5 times with 7.5 cm (3″) strip. Fasten off, weave in ends. Block. Add fringe if desired.

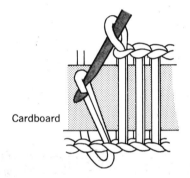

Cardboard

Long double crochet. Wool pulled up to height of cardboard to make chain stitch. Cardboard rests on top of previous row. Hold work in whatever position is most comfortable

Detail of yellow stole. Note how the long double crochet stitches are held secure between rows of double crochet

(Above) Pink stole made with chunky wool in Tunisian stitch simple and cluster stitch

(Right) Yellow stole made with chunky wool in long double crochet

Placemats and Curtains

The pieces in this section are good examples of how basic stitches can combine with the chain stitch to make a pattern. In all of the following, the chain stitch contributes greatly towards the final pattern. The blue placemat below combines double, treble, and double treble crochet to produce an original radial design. The green placemat on page 47 combines double and treble crochet and results in picots and a knobby texture. The pink placemat on page 47, with the Circle in Square motif (page 33), combines treble and double treble crochet and is worked in sections. The pink-red placemat (page 47) is treble crochet throughout. The curtain (page 46) is made by varying the pattern of the pink-red placemat slightly.

Blue placemat 42 cms×30.5 cms (16½″×12″), worked with carpet warp

four designs for placemats

PATTERN No. 1: Multiple of 13+6 ch.

Row 1: Tr in 4th ch from hook and in each ch across. Ch 3, turn.

Row 2: (Turning ch-3 counts as first tr) Tr in 2nd st, tr in each of next 2 sts, * ch 3, (sk 1 st, dble tr in next st)4×, ch 3, sk 1 st, tr in each of next 4 sts, rep from * across. Ch 3, turn.

Row 3: Tr in 2nd st, tr in each of next 2 sts, * ch 3, dc in each of next 4 dble tr, ch 3, tr in each of next 4 tr, rep from * across. Ch 3, turn.

Rows 4 & 5: Tr in 2nd st, tr in each of next 2 sts, * ch 3, dc in each of next 4 dc, ch 3, tr in each of next 4 tr, rep from * across. Ch 3, turn.

Row 6: Tr in 2nd st, tr in each of next 2 sts, * (ch 1, dble tr) in each of next 4 dc, ch 1, dc in each of next 4 tr, rep from * across. Ch 3, turn.

Row 7: Tr in 2nd st, tr in each st and ch across. Ch 3, turn.

Rep rows 2 to 7 for pattern.

TWO BLUE PLACEMATS, each 41.3 cms×30 cms (16½″×12″): Carpet warp (see page 80 for stockists), 450 metre (400 yd) spool. 3.00 crochet hook. Gauge: 6 tr = 2.5 cms (1″); 3 rows = 2.5 cms (1″). Ch 97, work row 1. Work patt rows 6×. Fasten off. Attach wool, work 2 rows dc around, 3 dc in each corner. Fasten off.

PATTERN No. 2: Picot lace. Multiple of 7+4 ch.

Row 1: Htr in 3rd ch from hook, htr in next ch, * ch 3, sk 2 ch, dc in next ch, ch 3, sk 2 ch, htr in each of next 2 ch, rep from * across. Ch 2, turn.

Row 2: Htr in each of first 2 htr, * ch 3, (1 dc, ch 3, 1 dc) in next dc, ch 3, htr in each of next w htr, rep from * across. Ch 1, turn.

Row 3: Dc in each of first 2 htr, * dc in ch-3 sp, ch 5, dc in next ch-3 sp, dc in each of next 2 htr, rep from * across. Ch 1, turn.

Row 4: Dc in each of first 2 dc, * 7 dc in ch-5 sp (arch), sk 1 dc, dc in each of next 2 dc, rep from * across. Ch 2, turn.

Row 5: Htr in each of first 2 dc, * ch 3, sk 3 dc, dc in next dc, ch 3, sk 3 dc, htr in each of next 2 dc, rep from * across. Ch 2, turn.

Rep rows 2 to 5 for pattern.

GREEN LINEN PLACEMAT, 44 cms×31 cms (17½″ × 12½″): Crochet cotton, four 25 gm (3 oz) balls. 5.00 crochet hook. Gauge: 3 patt reps across = 10 cms (4″). Ch 95, work row 1. Work patt rows until piece measures 30.5 cms (12″), end with row 5. Fasten off. Finish with 1 row dc around, 3 dc in each ch-3 sp, 3 dc in each corner. Join. Work 1 row reverse dc around.

PATTERN No. 3: See Circle in Square, page 33.

(Left) Detail of blue placemat showing double treble crochet in a radial pattern. (Right) Detail of green placemat showing picot loops

Detail of pink placemat (see page 47). Note how motifs are joined

PINK PLACEMAT, 42 cms × 29.2 cms ($16\frac{1}{2}'' × 11\frac{1}{2}''$): Crochet cotton, three 25 gm balls ($2\frac{1}{2}$ oz). 3.50 crochet hook. Work 6 motifs, each 13.5 cms ($5\frac{1}{4}''$) square. Block, sew tog, 3 across, 2 down. Attach wool to any ch-7 corner, work 5 dc in corner sp, 1 dc in each st around, 1 dc in each ch-1 sp, 5 dc in each ch-7 corner sp. Join to first st. Next row: Ch 3, try in 2nd st, 3 tr in next st (corner), * tr in each st around, 3 tr in each corner st, rep from * around. Fasten off.

PATTERN No. 4: Multiple of 20 + 12 ch.

Row 1: Tr in 4th ch from hook and in each of next 8 ch, * ch 10, sk 10 ch, tr in each of next 10 ch, rep from * across. Ch 3, turn.

Row 2: Tr in 2nd st (ch-3 counts as first tr), tr in each of next 8 sts, * ch 5, dc in ch-10 sp, ch 5, tr in each of next 10 tr, rep from * across. Ch 3, turn.

Row 3: Rep row 2, except change 'dc in ch-10 sp' to dc in dc of pr r.

Row 4: Tr in 2nd st and in each of next 8 sts, * ch 10, tr in each of next 10 tr, rep from * across. Turn.

Row 5: Ch 13, * 10 tr in ch-10 sp, ch 10, rep from *, ending tr in last tr of pr r. Turn.

Row 6: Ch 8, dc in ch-10 sp, ch 5, * tr in each of next 10 tr, ch 5, dc in ch-10 sp, ch 5, rep from *, ending tr in 11th ch of ch-13.

Row 7: Rep row 6, except change 'dc in ch-10 sp' to dc in dc of pr r. End row with tr in 6th ch of ch-8. Turn.

Row 8: Ch 13, * tr in each of next 10 tr, ch 10, rep from *, ending tr in top of ch-13. Ch 3, turn.

Row 9: 9 tr in ch-10 sp, * ch 10, 10 tr in next ch-10 sp, rep from * across. Ch 3, turn.

Rep rows 2 to 9 for pattern.

FOUR PINK-RED PLACEMATS, each 41 cms × 33 cms ($16'' × 13''$): Crochet cotton, twelve 25 gm balls (10 oz). 3.50 crochet hook. Gauge: 5 tr = 2.5 cms ($1''$); 3 rows = 2.5 cms ($1''$). Ch 72, work row 1. Work patt rows until piece measures 30.5 cms ($12''$), end with row 8. Fasten off. Finish with 1 row dc around, 8 dc in ch-10 sps. Block. Make 4 tassels, each 5 cms ($2''$) long, and attach.

CURTAIN (a variation on pattern No. 4): Crochet cotton, 75 gm (2 oz). 2.50 crochet hook. Gauge: 6 tr = 2.5 cms ($1''$); 5 rows = 5 cms ($2''$). Multiple of 22 + 12 ch. Ch 144 to start. 7 patt reps = 66 cms × 56 cms ($26'' × 22''$); further reps will add to width. To add to length, ch more to start or work separate pieces, then join. Follow patt No. 4 directions except inc all ch 5 and ch 8 by 1 ch, inc all other chs (except turning chs) by 2 chs. Row 1, for example, would be: Tr in 4th ch from hook and in each of next 8 ch, * ch 12, sk 12 ch, tr in each of next 10 ch, rep from * across. Finish same as placemat, minus tassels.

(Above) Curtain. A variation of pink-red placemat pattern turned vertically for hanging. (Below) Detail of above pattern shows long chains gathered in the centre by single crochet stitches

(Above) Green placemat, 44 cms×31 cms (17½″ ×12½″),
worked with 10/2 linen. (See page 45)

(Right) Pink placemat, 42 cms×29 cms (16½″ ×11½″),
Circle in Square motif

(Below) Pink-red placemat, 40.5 cms×33 cms (16″ ×
13″), worked with variegated wool

Cushion Covers

The traditional granny square makes a good beginner's project. It is used in the cushion covers on this page in two different colour combinations. The colours to the left, below, are placed in the same order throughout, whereas the ones below right are alternated. The rich surface of the cushion covers is the result of brilliant hues and velvety soft chenille yarn. The pinwheel cushion cover (facing page) uses the Tunisian stitch simple, thus creating a flat surface that does not conflict with the contemporary design – a design in which bands of colour, diamonds, and other geometric forms combine to give variety of shape. All the covers are worked in separate motifs that are joined at the finish.

Two cushion covers, 38 cms (15") square, worked in the granny motif, each in a different three-colour combination

Pinwheel cushion cover, 38 cms (15") square, worked in the Tunisian
stitch simple. Eight sections are made, four for each side

Granny motif, 13 cms (5″) square

2	3	2
3	1	3
2	3	2

Colour positions for Red, Pink and White cushion cover

granny cushion covers

Both cushion covers use chenille yarn (see page 80 for stockists). 5.00 crochet hook.

PATTERN STITCH: Granny square, follow directions on page 32. Each motif = 13 cms (5″) square.

YELLOW, ORANGE AND GREEN CUSHION COVER, 38 cms × 38 cms (15″ × 15″): Make 18 squares using the following wool amounts:

> 40.5 metres (135 ft) light yellow (colour A)
> 59.4 metres (198 ft) yellow (colour B)
> 79.2 metres (297 ft) orange (colour C)
> 121.5 metres (405 ft) green (colour D)

Weave in all ends at finish. Weave squares together, 3 across, 6 down. Fold work in half and weave tog on 2 sides, leaving one side open for cushion insertion. Insert cushion and sew opening closed. Either use a purchased cushion or make your own by cutting 2 pieces of fabric 43 cms (17″) square, seaming them together on three sides and stuffing with Kapok or shredded foam. Sew remaining side closed. For a variation, make squares for front of cushion only and finish the back with velveteen or other material.

RED, PINK AND WHITE CUSHION COVER, 38 cms × 38 cms (15″ × 15″): Make 18 squares using the following wool amounts:

> 70.5 metres (235 ft) dark red (colour A)
> 64.2 metres (214 ft) red (colour B)
> 54.3 metres (181 ft) pink (colour C)
> 121.5 metres (405 ft) white (colour D)

1. Make 2 squares, working rnd 1 in colour A, rnd 2 in colour B, rnd 3 in colour C, rnd 4 in colour D (Square 1).

2. Make 8 squares, working rnd 1 in colour B, rnd 2 in colour C, rnd 3 in colour A, rnd 4 in colour D (Square 2).

3. Make 8 squares, working rnd 1 in colour C, rnd 2 in colour A, rnd 3 in colour B, rnd 4 in colour D (Square 3).

Weave in ends. To finish, weave 9 squares together for front, placing A square in the centre, B squares in each corner, and C squares in remaining areas. Rep for back. Weave 3 sides together, leaving one open for cushion insertion. Insert; sew opening closed.

pinwheel cushion covers 38 cms × 38 cms (15″ × 15″)

Materials: Double knitting wool. 3.00 Tunisian hook.

125 gm (4 oz) turquoise	75 gm (2 oz) white
125 gm (4 oz) purple	75 gm (2 oz) black
125 gm (4 oz) medium blue	75 gm (2 oz) red
75 gm (2 oz) gold	

Gauge: 6 sts = 2.5 cms (1″); 5 rows = 2.5 cms (1″).

PATTERN STITCH: Tunisian stitch simple. Make 8 motifs in all. *Note:* Each row is worked in 2 steps (page 18 or 25). *Do not turn work throughout.*

TO MAKE MOTIF A: With turquoise, ch 40.

Row 1:

A. (Draw through a lp in top lp *only* of 2nd ch from hook and in each ch across.) Draw through first 5 ch with turquoise, next 3 ch with white, next 31 ch with turquoise.

B. With turquoise, wrh and through 1 lp on hook, * wrh and through 2 lps on hook, rep from * 30 × with turquoise, 3 × with white, 5 × with turquoise, once with purple.

Row 2:

A. Draw up a lp in 2nd vertical bar with turquoise, * draw up a lp in next vertical bar, rep from * 5 × with turquoise, 3 × with white, 29 × with turquoise, once with black.

B. With black, wrh and through 1 lp on hook, change to turquoise, * wrh and through 2 lps on hook, rep from * 28 more times with turquoise, 3 × with white, 6 × with turquoise, once with purple.

Rows 3–34: Follow colour changes on graph.

At end, sl st in each vertical bar across in matching colour.

Make two A motifs.

TO MAKE MOTIFS B, C, D: Make two of each. Follow graph for colour changes.

To finish, join motifs for each cushion half as shown. Sew 3 sides tog, leaving one side open for cushion insertion. Insert and sew closed.

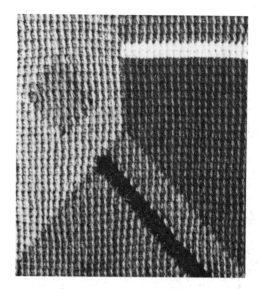

Pinwheel design. One section shown. Other sections are in same design, but different colours. See graph below

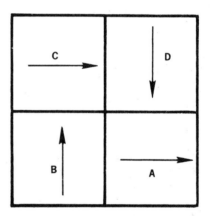

Position the sections as indicated by arrows, then join. Repeat for other side of cushion

GRAPH AND COLOURS FOR PINWHEEL DESIGN

Motif A and C	Motif B and D
1. Turquoise	1. Blue
2. White	2. Black
3. Purple	3. Purple
4. Blue	4. Gold
5. Gold (A), Purple (D)	5. Turquoise (B), Red (C)
6. Red	6. White
7. Gold	7. Turquoise
8. Black	8. Red

Note: With exception of diamond colours, sections A and D are in the same colours, as are sections B and C

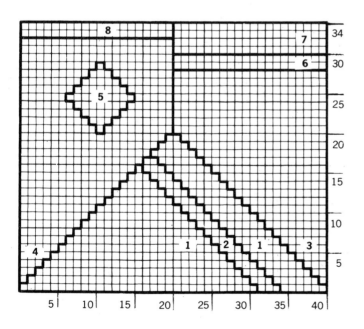

Baby's Blanket and Bedspreads

The solid-colour baby's blanket uses the delicate open shell stitch in an all-over pattern. It is ideal for crib or carriage. The basket bedspread (pictured on page 54), in a soft, smooth fabric, is worked with alternating colours in the Tunisian stitch simple. It is made in four long strips that are later joined. A double granny forms the centre of the multi-coloured bedspread (page 54). This is an ideal project for using up left-over wool. The star bedspread uses two motifs – the Octagon Swirl together with a joining motif. Chunky knitting wool is used in all.

Detail of baby's blanket showing open shell stitch

Detail of star bedspread showing Octagon Swirl motifs and joining motifs

baby's blanket 91 cms × 110 cms (36″ × 44″)

Materials: Chunky knitting wool, 550 gm (20 oz). 6.50 crochet hook.

Gauge: 3 shells = 13 cms (5″).

PATTERN STITCH: Lace shell. Multiple of 6+2 ch.

Ch 122 loosely.

Row 1: Dc in 2nd ch, dc in next ch, * ch 3, sk 3 ch, dc in each of next 3 ch, rep from *, ending dc in each of last 2 ch. Ch 1, turn.

Row 2: Dc in first st, * 5 tr in ch-3 sp (shell made), dc in 2nd dc, rep from * across. Turn.

Row 3: * Ch 3, 1 dc each in 2nd, 3rd, and 4th tr of shell, rep from *, ending ch 2, dc in last st. Ch 3, turn.

Row 4: 2 tr in ch-2 sp, * dc in 2nd dc, 5 tr in ch-3 sp (shell made), rep from *, ending dc in 2nd dc, 3 tr in ch-3 sp. Ch 1, turn.

Row 5: Dc in each of first 2 tr, * ch 3, 1 dc each in 2nd, 3rd, and 4th tr of shell, rep from *, ending tr in each of last 2 sts. Ch 1, turn.

Rep rows 2–5 until piece measures 102 cms (40″), then work 1 row dc around, 3 dc in each corner. Join with sl st, ch 1. *Do not turn.* Work 1 row htr, 3 htr in corners. Join with sl st. Sl st in each st around. Block.

star bedspread 168 cms × 122 cms (66″ × 48″)

Materials: Chunky knitting wool.
        4.50 crochet hook.
        125 gm (4 oz) dark gold (colour A)
        450 gm (16 oz) white (colour B)
        700 gm (24 oz) blue jewel (colour C)
        700 gm (24 oz) navy (colour D)

Gauge: Each star motif = 15 cms (6″); each joining motif = 6.5 cms (2½″) square.

PATTERN STITCH: Octagon Swirl, page 32. Make 88 motifs. Octagons leave spaces when joined; these are filled with joining motifs.

(Right) Baby's blanket, 91 cms×112 cms (36″×44″), in open shell stitch

Star bedspread, 168 cms×122 cms (66″×48″), Octagon Swirl motifs, in double knitting wool, individually made, then joined with a joining motif

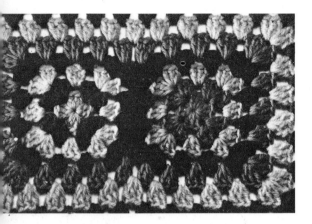

Two granny squares form centre of bedspread. Design grows row by row around motifs

JOINING MOTIF: With colour D ch 4, join with sl st to form ring.

Rnd 1: Ch 1, work 8 dc in ring. Join with sl st to first st.

Rnd 2: (Ch 3, 2 tr, ch 1, 3 tr) in first st, ch 1, sk 1 st, * (3 tr, ch 1, 3 tr) in next st, ch 1, sk 1 st, rep from * around. Sl st to top of ch-3.

Rnd 3: Sl st across 2 tr to ch-1 sp, (ch 3, 2 tr, ch 1, 3 tr) in same ch-1 sp, 3 tr in next ch-1 sp, * (3 tr, ch 1, 3 tr) in next ch-1 sp, 3 tr in next ch-1 sp, rep from * around. Join with sl st to top of ch-3. Fasten off. Make 70 motifs. Block and join with octagon motifs.

granny bedspread 173 cms × 158 cms (68″ × 62″)

Materials: Double knitting wool, approx. seventy-two 25 gm balls (64 oz) in various colours. 6.50 crochet hook.

Gauge: 3 tr = 2.5 cms (1″); 3 rows = 2.5 cms (1″).

Make 2 granny squares, following directions on page 32, and join. Working around squares, do tr in each ch-1 sp and (3 tr, ch 1, 3 tr) in each corner sp. Continue working around in this fashion, changing colour each row or in middle of row

Granny bedspread, 173 cms × 158 cms (68″ × 62″). Made with leftover double knitting wool

Basket bedspread, 122 cms (48″) square. Made with double knitting wool

GRAPH FOR BASKET BEDSPREAD

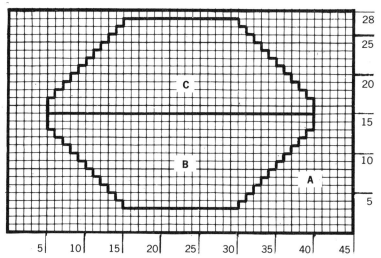

Repeat graph rows for each section. Note that basket colours reverse each time.

Detail of basket bedspread showing how rows are edged. Note that basket colours alternate

basket bedspread 122 cms × 122 cms (48″ × 48″)

Materials: Double knitting wool.

6.00 Tunisian hook. 5.50 crochet hook.

350 gm (12 oz) dark turquoise (colour A)

350 gm (12 oz) medium turquoise (colour B)

400 gm (14 oz) avocado (colour C)

Gauge: 5 sts = 2.5 cms (1″); 7 rows = 5 cms (2″).

TO MAKE ONE STRIP: With C, ch 45. Work rows 1–3 in Tunisian stitch simple.

Row 4:

A. Draw up a lp in 2nd vertical bar and in each of next 13 bars. Drop C, attach A and draw up a lp in each of next 15 bars, drop A, attach new strand of C and draw up a lp in each of next 15 bars.

B. Work off lps with C until 2nd lp on hook is colour A, change to A and work off 15 sts, change to C and work off remainder of sts.

Rows 5–28: Follow colour changes on graph.

Rep rows 1–28 five more times. After last row, work 1 row with C (2nd half of row is sl st in 2nd bar and in each bar across). Fasten off. Make 3 more strips. Block. With A and size 5.00 hook, work 1 tr row on long edges of 2 strips (they will form centre of bedspread). On other 2 strips work tr row only on the long edges that will face inside. Attach B, work 1 tr row on A edges. Sew strips tog along their lengths. Attach A, work 2 tr rows all around, attach B and work 1 tr row. Fasten off.

Pot-holders

You can have as much fun making these gaily detailed pot-holders as others will have looking at them. The ladybird, frog, butterfly, and apple are crocheted in rug wool to ensure protection against hot handles. The use of heavy wool, together with a few simple stitches, ensures that the work will go quickly. These are good projects for leftover wool and for gift-giving.

These pot-holders were made with uncut rug wool left over from other projects.

Materials: Approx. two 50 gm balls (3½ oz) of each colour. 4.50 crochet hook.

Gauge: 8 dc = 7.5 cms (3″); 3 rows = 2.5 cms (1″).

Note: Abbreviation eon = each of next.

butterfly approx. 21.5 cms × 18 cms (8½″ × 7″)

Colours: Turquoise (A), pink (B), green (C), white (D), black (E).

RIGHT WING OF BUTTERFLY: With A, ch 14.

Row 1: (right side) Dc in 2nd ch from hook and in each ch across, ch 1, turn.

Row 2: Dc across, end 2 dc in last st, ch 1, turn.

Row 3: 2 dc in first st, dc in eon 12 sts, 2 dc in last st, ch 1, turn.

Rows 4 & 5: Rep row 2.

Row 6: Dc in each st across, end 1 dc dec (page 16 or 23) in last 2 sts, ch 1, turn.

Row 7: Dec 1 dc, dc in next st and in each st across, end 2 dc in last st, ch 1, turn.

Row 8: Dc in each of first 2 sts, htr in eon 4 sts, dc in eon 4 sts, sl st across next 2 sts, dc in next st, htr in next st, tr in eon 2 sts, dc in next st. Fasten off.

(Right side) Attach B to right edge of 5th row, ch 1, 1 htr on row 6 edge, 1 tr on row 7 edge. On row 8, work 1 tr on edge, 2 htr in first st, htr in next st, dc in next st, sl st in next st. Fasten off.

(Right side) Attach C to 3rd B st on right edge, ch 1, dc in next st, htr in eon 2 sts, dc in next st, sl st in next st. Fasten off.

(Right side) Attach B to 11th A st from left edge, ch 1, dc in eon 4 sts, htr in eon 4 sts, tr in eon 2 sts. Fasten off.

Attach C in st just before first B st, ch 1, dc in ch-1 of B row, dc in eon 4 sts, htr in eon 4 sts, tr in eon 2 sts. Fasten off.

LEFT WING OF BUTTERFLY: Rep rows 1 to 8 as for right wing. Row 2 will be right side. With right side facing, attach wools as before, but to left edge.

To finish: Ch 2 with E. With wrong sides facing, join wings with 1 row dc through both A edges. Ch 9 and join ch to last dc for loop. Weave ends. Block.

Embroider a circle with D in upper and lower parts of each wing, and one down the centre with C.

ladybird 24 cms (9½″) circumference

Colours: Red (A), black (B), yellow (C). *Note:* 'Work over' wool for colour changes, see page 27.

With A, ch 6, join with sl st to form ring.

Rnd 1: Ch 1, 8 dc in centre of ring. Join with sl st.

Rnd 2: Ch 1, 2 dc in each st around. Join with sl st.

Rnd 3: Ch 1, * *with A* (dc in next st, 2 dc in next st) 2×, dc in next st, *attach B*, with B work 2 dc in next st, rep from * once more, *with A* (dc in next st, 2 dc in next st)2×. Join.

Two pot-holders: apple and frog

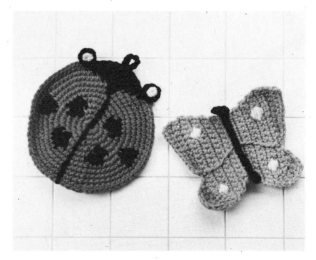

Two pot-holders: ladybird and butterfly

Rnd 4: Ch 1, dc in next st. *With B*, 2 dc in next st, *with A* dc in eon 2 sts, 2 dc in next st, *with B* dc in next st, 2 dc in next st, dc in eon 2 sts, *with A* 2 dc in next st, dc in eon 2 sts, 2 dc in next st, dc in next st, *with B* dc in next st, 2 dc in next st, dc in eon 2 sts, *with A* dc in next st, 2 dc in next st, dc in next st, *with B* 2 dc in next st, *with A* dc in next st, 2 dc in next st. Join.

Rnd 5: *With B* ch 1, 2 dc in first st, dc in eon 2 sts, *with A* dc in next st, 2 dc in next st, dc in eon 2 sts, *with B* dc in next st, 2 dc in next st, dc in next st, *with A* dc in eon 2 sts, 2 dc in next st, dc in eon 3 sts, 2 dc in next st, dc in eon 2 sts, *with B* dc in next st, 2 dc in next st, dc in next st, *with A* dc in eon 2 sts, 2 dc in next st, *with B* dc in eon 2 sts, 2 dc in next st, dc in next st, *with A* dc in eon 4 sts. Join *with B*.

Rnd 6: *With B* ch 1, dc in eon 4 sts, *with A* (2 dc, dc in eon 4 sts)5×, 2 dc in next st, dc in eon 2 sts, *with B* dc in eon 4 sts, *with A* 2 dc in next st, dc in eon 4 sts. Join.

Rnd 7: Ch 1, dc in eon 5 sts, *with B* 2 dc in next st, *with A* dc in eon 2 sts, 2 dc in next st, dc in eon 10 sts, *with B* 2 dc in next st, *with A* dc in eon 6 sts, 2 dc in next st, dc in eon 6 sts, *with B* dc in eon 2 sts, *with A* dc in next st, 2 dc in next st, dc in eon 8 sts, 2 dc in next st, dc in eon 2 sts. Join.

Rnd 8: Ch 1, dc in eon 4 sts, *with B* 2 dc in next st, dc in eon 2 sts, *with A* dc in eon 4 sts, 2 dc in next st, dc in eon 8 sts, *with B* 2 dc in next st, dc in eon 2 sts, *with A* dc in eon 7 sts, 2 dc in next st, dc in eon 5 sts, *with B* dc in next st, 2 dc in next st, dc in next st, *with A* dc in eon 8 sts, 2 dc in next st, dc in eon 7 sts. Join.

Rnd 9: Ch 1, dc in eon 4 sts, *with B* 2 dc in next st, dc in eon 2 sts, *with A* dc in eon 13 sts, *with B* dc in eon 7 sts, *with A* dc in eon 12 sts, *with B* dc in eon 4 sts, *with A* dc in eon 18 sts. Join.

Rnd 10: Ch 1, dc in eon 19 sts, *with B* dc in eon 4 sts, 2 dc in next st, dc in eon 5 sts, *with A* dc in eon 33 sts. Join.

Rnd 11: Ch 1, dc in first st, (2 dc in next st, dc in eon 6 sts)2×, dc in next 2 sts, *with B* sl st across next st, dc in eon 2 sts, htr in eon 7 sts, dc in eon 3 sts, sl st across next st, *with A* dc in next st, (2 dc in next st, dc in eon 7 sts)3×, 2 dc in next st, dc in eon 6 sts. Join. Fasten off.

EYES (make 2): With C ch 2, work 5 tr in 2nd ch from hook, join with sl st. Fasten off. Attach B and sl st in each st around. Fasten off.

To finish: Block. With B embroider a row down the centre. Sew an eye at each end of B at top. For loop attach B to centre top, ch 9, sl st to beginning. Weave in ends.

frog   approx. 21.5 cms × 18 cms (8½″ × 7″)

Colours: Yellow (A), chartreuse (B), green (C), 0.9 metres (1 yd) orange (D).

BODY: With A, ch 16.

Row 1: Htr in 3rd ch from hook, htr in eon 5 ch, dc in eon 2 ch, htr in eon 6 ch. Ch 2, turn.

Rows 2–6: Htr in each of first 6 sts, dc in eon 2 sts, htr in eon 6 sts. Ch 2, turn.

Rows 7 & 8: Sk first st (dec), work htr in htr and dc in dc across, end sk next to last st (dec).

Row 9: Htr in each of first 4 sts, dc in eon 2 sts, htr in eon 4 sts. Fasten off.

HEAD: Ch 4 with B, insert hook in last row of body, work dc in each st across (10 sts), ch 4, turn.

Row 2: Dc in 2nd ch from hook, htr in eon 2 ch, tr in eon 10 sts, htr in eon 2 ch, dc in next ch, sl st to last ch. Attach C, ch 1. Break off B.

Rows 3 & 4: Sl st in first st, dc in next st, htr in eon 2 sts, tr in eon 10 sts, htr in eon 2 sts, dc in next st, sl st to turning ch. Ch 1, turn.

Row 5: Sl st across first 4 sts, dc in eon 10 sts, sl st across last 4 sts. Fasten off.

With right side facing, attach A, work 1 row sl st around yellow sides.

LEGS (make 2): Ch 13 with C, dc in 2nd ch from hook, dc in next ch, htr in each of next 2 ch, tr in eon 7 ch, htr in last ch. Fasten off.

EYES (make 2): Ch 4 with D, join with sl st, ch 2, work 8 htr in ring, join with sl st. Break off. Attach C, ch 1, sl st loosely around. Fasten off.

To finish, match narrow ends of legs to 3rd A row and sew to body so that wide ends extend 1.3 cms (½″) below A rows. With D, cut four 10 cm (4″) strands, and double knot two to each end of leg. Sew eyes to head. To make loop, attach B between eyes, ch 18, sl st in same sp as attached. Fasten off, weave in ends. Block.

apple   approx. 21.5 cms × 18 cms (8½″ × 7″)

Colours: White (A), light yellow (B), yellow (C), red (D), dark green (E).

FIRST HALF: With A, ch 16.

Row 1: Dc in 2nd ch from hook, dc in next ch and in each ch across (15 sts), ch 1, turn.

Row 2: Sl st across first 5 sts, ch 1, dc in next st, tr in eon 3 sts, dc in next st, sl st across last 5 sts. With B ch 1, turn.

Row 3: Dc in eon 5 sl sts, htr in next st, tr in eon 3 sts, htr in next st, dc in last 5 sl sts, ch 1, turn.

Row 4: Sl st across first 5 sts, ch 1, dc in next st, htr in next st, tr in eon 2 sts, htr in next st, dc in next st, sl st across last 5 sts, attach C, ch 1, turn.

Row 5: 2 dc in first sl st, dc in eon 2 sts, htr in eon 3 sts, tr in eon 4 sts, htr in eon 3 sts, dc in eon 2 sts, 2 dc in last st, ch 1, turn.

Row 6: 2 dc in first st, dc in eon 3 sts, htr in eon 3 sts, tr in next st, 2 tr in next st, tr in eon 2 sts, htr in eon 3 sts, dc in eon 3 sts, 2 dc in last st, ch 1, turn.

Row 7: Dc in first st, htr in eon 2 sts, tr in eon 15 sts, htr in eon 2 sts, dc in last st. Fasten off.

SECOND HALF: Make the same as first half.

Join halves by sewing together with A. With right side facing, attach D to bottom, just before first B st, ch 1, work 1 row dc around edge, ending at A on bottom. Attach D to top edge, ch 1, dc work htr across top, dec 1 st when working over A, end dc, sl st across last 2 sts on left edge. For loop, attach A to top, ch 10, join where attached. Fasten off. Block.

LEAF: With E, ch 10, dc in 2nd ch from hook, htr in eon 2 ch, tr in eon 3 ch, htr in eon 2 ch, dc in last ch. Ch 1, turn.

Row 2: Dc in first st, htr in eon 2 sts, tr in eon 3 sts, htr in eon 2 sts, dc in last st. Fasten off. Sew to top of apple.

With E, embroider a row down the centre between A and B, then between B and C. With black, make 4 or 5 French knots for seeds.

Butterfly design pot-holder crocheted with rug wool

Pot-holders can also be used as wall decorations to brighten up the kitchen. Shown are three designs: ladybird, frog and apple

Rugs

The rugs on this page, one looped, the other flat, are made in diamond-shaped sections of light and dark colours. When finished, these sections can be joined in any combination. Both rugs are worked in variations of a simple increase/decrease pattern, the looped one around a cardboard strip. Because different techniques are used in making the rugs, each produces a contrasting texture. Yet another texture can be seen in the striped rug (page 63). Here heavy wool is used double throughout in a crossed double crochet stitch and is crocheted quickly on a jumbo-sized hook. The use of doubled wool gives body to the piece and increases its wearability. All three projects are good as experiments for combining colours.

(Left) Diamond sections in double crochet loop stitch. Join to form rug

(Below) Diamond sections worked in half treble crochet. Can be joined to form rug, or other items such as bedspread or placemat

loop diamond rug

Materials: Uncut rug wool.
One 64 metre (70 yd) skein makes 3 diamonds.
5.00 crochet hook.
1 cardboard strip, 2.5 cms (1″) wide, any length.

Gauge: 3 sts = 2.5 cms (1″); 3 rows = 2.5 cms (1″).

TO MAKE ONE DIAMOND, 9 cms × 21.5 cms ($3\frac{1}{2}″ × 8\frac{1}{2}″$): Ch 2 to begin.

Row 1: (right side) Dc in 2nd ch from hook, ch 1, turn.

Row 2: (Insert hook into first st, hold cardboard strip at back of work and against pr r, wrap wool around strip, wrh and draw through a lp, wrh and draw through 2 lps on hook – loop st made)2×. Rep for next st, ch 1, turn. Remove cardboard.

Row 3: Dc in each dc across, ch 1, turn.

Row 4: 2 lp sts in first st, 1 lp st in next st and in each st across, ending 2 lp sts in last st, ch 1, turn.

Row 5: Same as row 3.

Rep rows 4 and 5 for pattern.

Work pattern rows until there are 14 lps. Work 1 row dc across, then, continuing in pattern, dec 1 lp at beg and end of each lp st row until 4 lps remain. Work 2 dc in one. Fasten off. **To dec lp st:** (insert hook into next st, wrap wool around strip, wrh and draw through a lp)2×, wrh and through 3 lps on hook. Make as many diamonds as desired and join (see page 62 for suggested patterns). Edges can be squared off if desired by making triangles and adding where needed.

If you wish to make rectangular shapes instead of diamond ones, ch desired length and work as follows:

Row 1: Dc in 2nd ch from hook, and in each ch across, ch 1, turn.

Row 2: Make a lp st in first st and in each st across, ch 1, turn.

Row 3: Dc in first st and in each st across, ch 1, turn.

Rep rows 2 and 3 for pattern.

The diamond principle can be applied to a flat rug (without loops), or to a bedspread made with finer yarn. (The sample, page 60 bottom, was made with rug wool, and a 4.00 crochet hook; 100 gm [3 oz] makes 10 diamonds; gauge, 4 htr = 2.5 cms [1″]: 6 rows = 5 cms [2″].) To make one diamond, ch 3.

Row 1: Htr in 3rd ch from hook, ch 2, turn.

Row 2: 2 htr in st, ch 2, turn.

Row 3: 2 htr in each st, ch 2, turn.

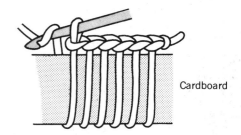

Working loop stitch over cardboard strip. Hold horizontally or vertically

Flat-stitch diamond   Loop-stitch diamond

36 diamond sections

Row 4: 2 htr in first st, htr in each of next 2 sts, 2 htr in last st, ch 2, turn.

Continue to inc at end of each row until there are 20 sts.

Next row: Wrh and draw a lp through first st, keep lp on hook, wrh and draw a lp through 2nd st, wrh and through 5 lps on hook (1 htr dec), htr in each st across to last 2 sts, wrh and draw a lp through next to last st, wrh and draw a lp through last st, wrh and through 5 lps on hook (1 htr dec). Ch 2, turn.

Continue to dec at each end until 1 st remains, ch 1. Fasten off.

40 diamond sections

Two design arrangements for diamond sections. For squared off edges, add triangles. Triangles and diamonds can be combined or worked alone for a variety of patchwork designs

striped rug   66 cms × 102 cms (26″ × 40″)

Materials: Uncut rug wool.
        7.50 crochet hook.
        300 gm (10½ oz) tangerine (colour A)
        250 gm (8¾ oz) bright yellow (colour B)
        150 gm (5 oz) dark gold (colour C)

Gauge: 3 dc = 5 cms (2″); 5 rows = 10 cms (4″).

PATTERN STITCH: Crossed dc. Chain is an uneven number. *Note:* Use two strands as one throughout.

With 2 strands of colour A, ch 41.

Row 1: Dc in 2nd ch from hook and in each ch across (40 sts). Ch 1, turn.

Row 2: Sk first st, dc in 2nd st, dc in skipped st (crossed dc made), * sk 1 st, dc in next st, dc in sk st, rep from * across, ch 1, turn.

Row 3: Dc in each st across, ch 1, turn.

Row 4: Rep row 2.

Row 5: Rep row 3 except on last wrh of row drop 1 strand A, add 1 strand B.

Rep rows 2 and 3 for pattern.

Work in pattern with the following colours:

5 rows with A & B	5 rows with A & B
5 rows with B	3 rows with B
5 rows with B & C	3 rows with B & C
5 rows with C	3 rows with C
5 rows with C & A	3 rows with C & A
5 rows with A	3 rows with A

Fasten off, weave in ends. Block.

Detail of striped rug. Note directions of crossed double crochet stitches

Striped rug, 66 cms×102 cms (26″×40″). The use of doubled wool forms
a thick, sturdy rug and allows for the blending of colours

Soft white raffia hat with ribbon

Hats and Ski Band

The white hat on the facing page is worked in raffia straw; its brim dips softly as here or can curve upward to frame the face. The feather-weight straw makes the hat ideal for summer wear. The dominant stitch is treble crochet worked in rounds; filet mesh provides the space for ribbon insertion. Double and half treble crochet are combined in the ski band. Motifs are sewn onto the ear-flaps for a light contrasting touch. The tri-colour hat is crocheted in alternating bands and strips. The stitch is raised treble crochet worked in tall triangular sections that are joined when finished.

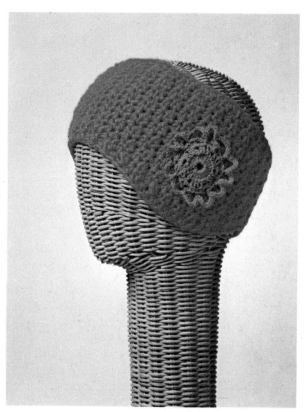

(Above) Ski band with attached motifs in contrasting colour. Motif for one side is shown

(Left) The tri-colour hat is shown standing up straight so that alternating design can be seen

raffia hat

Materials: Raffia, three 67.5 metre (75 yd) spools. 4.00 crochet hook. 137 cms of ribbon, 1 cm wide (1½ yds of ½″ ribbon).

Gauge: 4 tr = 2.5 cms (1″); 3 tr rows = 5 cms (2″).

PATTERN STITCH: Tr in rounds.

Ch 5, join with sl st to form ring.

Rnd 1: Ch 3 (counts as first st), work 11 tr in ring (12 tr), join with sl st to top of ch-3.

Rnd 2: Ch 3, 1 tr in join, 2 tr in each st around (24 tr), join to top of ch-3.

Rnd 3: Ch 3, * 2 tr in next st, 1 tr in next st, rep from * around (36 tr), join to top of ch-3.

Rnd 4: Ch 3, * 2 tr in next st, 1 tr in each of next 2 sts, rep from * around (48 tr), join to top of ch-3.

Rnd 5: Ch 3, * 2 tr in next st, 1 tr in each of next 3 sts, rep from * around (60 tr), join to top of ch-3.

Rnd 6: Ch 3, * 2 tr in next st, 1 tr in each of next 4 sts, rep from * around (72 tr), join to top of ch-3.

Rnd 7: Ch 3, 1 tr in each st around (72 tr), join to top of ch-3.

Rep rnd 7 four more times.

Next rnd: (Filet mesh) Ch 4, * sk 1 st, 1 tr in next st, ch 2, rep from * around, join to top of ch-3.

BRIM:

Rnd 1: Ch 3, * 4 tr in next ch-2 sp of pr r, 3 tr in next ch-2 sp of pr r, rep from * around, join to top of ch-3.

Rnd 2: Ch 3, tr in each st around, join to top of ch-3. Turn.

Rnds 3 & 4: Same as rnd 2.

Rnd 5: (Filet mesh) Ch 4, * sk next st, tr in next st, ch 1, rep from * around, join to 3rd ch of ch-4.

Rnd 6: Ch 3, * tr in ch-1 sp, tr in next st, rep from * around, join to top of ch-3. Fasten off.

Insert ribbon through first filet mesh rnd and tie in a bow.

ski band with motif

Materials: Double knitting wool, 75 gm (2 oz). 6.00 crochet hook.

Gauge: 4 sts = 2.5 cms (1″); 10 rows = 7.5 cms (3″).

PATTERN STITCH: Dc over htr. Chain is an uneven number.

Starting at the back, ch 11.

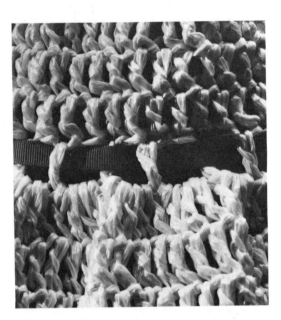

Detail of raffia hat showing ribbon inserted through a filet mesh row

Row 1: Dc in 2nd ch from hook, htr in next ch, * dc in next ch, htr in next ch, rep from * across (10 sts). Ch 1, turn.

Row 2: Dc in first st, htr in next st, * dc in next st, htr in next st, rep from * across. Ch 1, turn.

Rep row 2 until piece measures 5 cms (2″).

FIRST EAR-FLAP:

Row 1: Dc, htr in first st (inc made), dc in next st, * htr in next st, dc in next st, rep from * across. Ch 1, turn.

Keeping in pattern, inc on same edge every row for 2 rows. Keeping in pattern, inc on same edge every *other* row for 4 rows. Work even (without inc or dec) for 5 rows. Keeping in pattern, dec one st every other row for 4 rows. Then work even until piece measures 30 cms (12″). Front of ski band made.

SECOND EAR-FLAP: Keeping in pattern, inc 1 st every row on shaped edge for 4 rows, work even for 5 rows, dec 1 st every other row on shaped edge for 2 rows, dec 2 sts every row on shaped edge for 3 rows, work even for 5 cms (2″). Fasten off. Sew back seam. If desired, adapt any motif in book and sew one on each ear-flap. (See photo, page 65.) Use crochet cotton and 5.00 steel crochet hook.

tri-colour hat

Materials: Double knitting wool, 75 gm (2 oz) each: black (A), red (B), green (C).
4.50 crochet hook.

Gauge: 5 tr = 2.5 cms (1″); 6 rows = 5 cms (2″).

PATTERN STITCH: Raised tr. Chain is an even number.

With A, ch 20.

Row 1: Tr in 2nd ch from hook and in each ch across, ch 3, turn.

Row 2: Tr in 2nd st and in each st across, ch 1, turn.

Row 3: Dc in first st, * dc under bar of next tr (diag.), dc in next st, rep from * across. Ch 3, turn.

Rep rows 2 and 3 for pattern. Work in pattern for 6 cms (2½″), change to B, work 2 rows, change to A, work 5 cms (2″), change to C. Working in pattern with C, dec one st at beg and end of every 6th row. When C measures 16.5 cms (6½″), change to B, work 2 rows, change to C. Continue to dec every 6th row until 3 sts remain. Fasten off. Make 4 more triangles, varying colour positions and placements of stripes.

To finish, block triangles and sew together. Weave a doubled strand through top of hat, pull to tighten, then knot. Attach A to bottom row and work dc around. Dec 5 sts on each row, work 2 more rows with A, 3 rows with C. With B, work 3 rows even. Fasten off. Make tassel with the three colours and attach to top.

Detail of ski band showing double and half treble crochet stitches combined in a pattern

Detail of tri-colour hat showing ridge design of raised treble crochet

Working under treble crochet bar. Hook shows direction of stitch

Hat and Scarf Sets

Variegated chunky knitting wool and the cluster stitch combine to give a highly textured look to the pink hat and scarf set on the facing page. The hat is worked in rounds; the scarf in short rows. In the red and navy set, the hat is worked widthways like a narrow scarf and is seamed together at the finish; the scarf is crocheted lengthways on a long chain. Both are done in a double crochet ridge stitch.

variegated hat

Materials: Chunky knitting wool, 125 gm (4 oz). 6.50 crochet hook.

Gauge: 3 clusters = 5 cms (2″); 2 rows = 5 cms (2″).

PATTERN STITCH: Cluster (cl) in rnds. (*Note:* Pull up a long first lp in each tr.)

Ch 5, join to form ring.

Rnd 1: Ch 3, work 8 tr in ring, join to top of ch-3.

Rnd 2: Ch 3, work 2 tr in sp between each tr (cl), end tr in last sp (9 cls), join to top of ch-3.

Rnd 3: Ch 3, * sk 1 tr, cl in next sp, sk 2 tr, cl in next sp, rep from * around, end tr in join sp. Join to top of ch-3.

Rnd 4: Ch 3, * (sk 2 tr, cl in next sp)2×, (sk 1 tr, cl in next sp) 2×, rep from *, end tr in join sp. Join to top of ch-3.

Rnds 5–8: Rep row 4, except work first half of rep as follows: 3× for rnd 5, 4× for rnd 6, 5× for rnd 7, 6× for rnd 8. (2nd half of rep is worked 2× throughout.)

Rnds 9–12: Ch 3, work (sk 2 tr, cl in next sp) around, end tr in join sp. Join to top of ch-3.

Rnd 13: Ch 1, work dc in each st around. Join.

Work 4 more dc rnds, dec 3 sts evenly each rnd. Fasten off. Make pompon and sew to top of hat.

variegated scarf

25.5 cms × 153 cms (10″ × 60″) (excluding fringe)

Chunky knitting wool, 225 gm (8 oz). Same hook and gauge as hat. Pull up tr lp as above.

Ch 28 to start.

Row 1: Tr in 4th ch from hook and in each ch across, ch 3, turn.

Row 2: Sk 1 tr, tr in next sp, (sk 2 tr, 2 tr in next sp) across, ch 3, turn.

Row 3: (sk 2 tr, 2 tr in next sp) across, end tr in top of ch-3.

Rep rows 2 and 3 until piece measures 153 cms (60″), or desired length. Fasten off. Add a fringe 15 cms (6″) long at each end.

red and navy hat

Materials: Chunky knitting wool, 75 gm (2 oz) each: red and navy. 7.00 crochet hook.

Gauge: 3 dc = 2.5 cms (1″); 4 rows = 2.5 cms (1″).

PATTERN STITCH: Dc ridge st.

With navy, ch 28.

Row 1: Dc in 2nd ch and in each ch across, ch 1, turn.

Row 2: Dc in *back* lp of each st across, ch 1, turn.

Row 3: Rep row 2.

Row 4: Dc in back lp of first st, * dc in back lp of next st, rep from * 21× (shaping of hat). Ch 1, turn.

Row 5: Dc in back lp across. Attach red, ch 1, turn.

Row 6: With red rep row 2 including sts not worked on row 4.

Rows 7–9: Rep row 2, working rows 8–9 in navy.

Rep rows 4–9 as follows: 6 red rows, 4 navy, 4 red, 6 navy, 2 red, 4 navy, 4 red, 2 navy, 6 red, 4 navy, 4 red, 6 navy, 2 red, 4 navy, 6 red, 2 navy, 6 red.

Sew first and last rows tog. Weave a doubled strand through end st of each long row, draw tight and fasten. To make band, attach navy to back seam, work 1 dc rnd (53 sts), join to first st. Turn to wrong side and work dc under bar of next dc (work as in diagram on page 67) for 5 rnds. Fasten off. Make pompon and sew to hat.

red and navy scarf

183 cms × 20.5 cms (72″ × 8″) (with fringe)

Same materials (125 gm [4 oz] each colour) and gauge as hat. With navy, make a ch 153 cms (60″) long. Work rows 1 and 2 as for hat. Rep row 2 for 4 more navy rows, then work 4 red rows, 2 navy, 6 red, 4 navy, 2 red, 2 navy. Fasten off. Add a 15 cm (6″) fringe to each end.

(Right) Red and navy matching hat and scarf. (Below) Matching hat and scarf crocheted with variegated wool

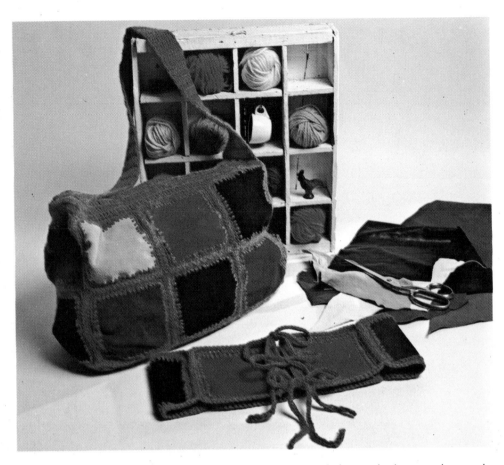

Suede handbag and matching belt are made by crocheting together suede squares of different colours

Clutch handbag and belt of rattail rayon

Shoulder bag with flower motifs

Bags and Belts

The handbag and matching belt on the facing page are made of plain square shapes cut out of suede (leather can also be used). The texture and pattern of the crochet stitches used to join the pieces contrast well with the smooth or shiny surfaces of the squares. A good use for scrap materials and leftover wools. (Facing page, below left) Satiny rattail rayon provides a touch of elegance to this clutch handbag and belt worked in the very interesting double crochet weave. The bag is made in one piece. The white shoulder bag, worked in a variation of the cluster stitch, uses heavy rug wool and a jumbo-sized hook. Small motifs are crocheted separately and sewn on for colour accent.

suede handbag

Materials: Nineteen 10 cm (4″) squares of suede or leather. Double knitting wool, 150 gm (5 oz), copper or heather (for bag *and* belt). 3.50 crochet hook. Awl or leather punch. 30 cm (12″) zipper.

With awl or leather punch make holes around each square 3 mms ($\frac{1}{8}$″) from edge, 5 mms ($\frac{1}{4}$″) apart. Attach yarn to any hole and work as follows:

Rnd 1: Work dc in each hole, 3 dc in each corner hole. Join with sl st to first st. Do not turn.

Rnds 2 & 3: Dc in each st, 3 dc in each corner st. Join with sl st to first st. Do not turn.

Fasten off. Sew squares together as shown.

FLAPS: With right side facing, work 1 dc row across top 3 squares at front of bag, ch 3, turn. Tr in 2nd st, tr in each st across, ch 3, turn. Work 4 more tr rows. Fasten off. Rep for back of bag. Sew flaps to end sides and sew zipper along centre of both flaps.

STRAP: Work 1 tr row across end square of one side, continue working tr rows, dec at each end until 10 tr remain. Work even on 10 tr until strap measures 86 cms (34″), or desired length, inc 1 tr at each end until there are 20 tr. Fasten off. Sew to end square of other side.

suede belt

Five 10 cm (4″) squares make a 50 cm (26″) belt. Work squares as for bag and sew tog. Make six 30 cm (12″) lengths of treble ch. Sew to belt for tying.

Detail of suede squares. Note edgings of double crochet rows and the manner of joining

PATTERN FOR HANDBAG – 19 squares
Crochet for flap

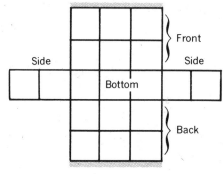

Crochet for flap

clutch handbag 25.5 cms × 38 cms (10″ × 15½″)

Materials: Rattail rayon (see page 80 for stockists). 4.00 crochet hook.
Size 4 fastener. 30 cm (12″) length of hat wire.
99 metres (110 yds) colour A; 49.5 metres (55 yds) colour B;
10.8 metres (12 yds) colour C.

Gauge: 7 dc = 5 cms (2″); 4 rows = 2.5 cms (1″).

PATTERN STITCH: Double crochet weave. Chain is an even number.

With A, ch 36.

Row 1: Working over hat wire, dc in 2nd ch from hook and in each ch across (35 sts). Ch 1, turn.

Row 2: Attach B (tie to A strand). Keeping B at back of work, dc in first st with A, * bring B to front of work, dc in next st with A, bring B to back of work across dc just made. Keeping B in back, dc in next st with A (thus weaving B in front and back of A), rep from * across. Ch 1, turn.

Row 3: Bring B around edge to back of work, dc in first st with A, * bring B to front, dc in next st with A, bring B to back across dc just made, dc in next st with A, rep from * across. Ch 1, turn.

Rep row 3 for 2.5 cms (1″) except, for A read C. Fasten off.
With B, ch 1, turn. Dc in next st and in each st across. Ch 1, turn. Work dc rows for 5 cms (2″). Work last ch 1 with C.

Next row: Keeping B in back, dc in first st with C, * bring B to front, dc in next st with C, bring B to back across dc just made. Keeping B in back, dc in next st with C, rep from * across, ch 1, turn.

Rep row 3 for 2.5 cms (1″) except, for A read C. Fasten off.

To finish, weave in ends, fold wire ends and sew over them to keep in place. Fold bottom half of piece to the point where colour B begins. Sew side seams. Fold top over for flap, sew fastener under flap and in the centre.

Detail of clutch handbag showing pattern of double crochet weave

belt

Materials: Rattail rayon No. 2 (see page 80 for stockists). 4.00 crochet hook. 5 cm (2″) buckle.
45 metres (50 yds) colour A; 9 metres (10 yds) colour B;
4.5 metres (5 yds) colour C.

For a belt 5 cms × 76 cms (2″ × 30″), ch 8 with colour A, work rows 1 to 3 as for purse, rep row 3 for pattern until piece measures 71 cms (28″). Work 5 cms (2″) of dc with B. Work 2.5 cms (1″) in dc weave with B and C. To finish, sew buckle to belt.

white shoulder bag 30 cms × 35 cms (12″ × 14″)

Materials: Uncut rug wool, three 63 metre (70 yd) skeins.
7.50 crochet hook.

Gauge: 1 cluster = 2.5 cms (1″).

PATTERN STITCH: Variation of cluster (cl). Multiple of 2+5 ch.

Ch 29 for one side of bag.

Row 1: (right side) Draw up lp in 2nd ch from hook and in each of next 3 ch (5 lps on hook), wrh and pull through 5 lps on hook (cluster made), ch 1 (eye of cl), * insert hook into eye and pull through lp, insert hook into last ch of previous cl and pull through lp, pull up a lp in each of next 2 ch (5 lps on hook), wrh and pull through 5 lps on hook, ch 1, rep from * across. Ch 1, turn.

Row 2: Dc in first ch (eye) and in each st and ch across. Ch 3, turn.

Row 3: Pull up 1 lp each in 2nd and 3rd ch of ch-3, pull up lp in each of first 2 sts (5 lps on hook), wrh and pull through 5 lps on hook, ch 1, * pull up lp in eye, pull up lp in last st of previous cl, pull up lp in each of next 2 sts, wrh and pull through 5 lps on hook, ch 1, rep from * across. Ch 1, turn.

Rep rows 2 and 3 for 13 more rows. Fasten off. Make other side of bag exactly the same.

GUSSET AND HANDLE: Ch 7, work in pattern until piece measures 102 cms (40″). Fasten off. Sew to both sides of bag.

Detail of shoulder bag shows clustering of stitches

FLOWER MOTIF: With leftover double knitting wool, ch 5, join with sl st to form ring. In centre of ring work (1 dc, ch 4, 1 dble tr, ch 4)6×. Sl st to first dc. Fasten off. Make as many as you wish and sew onto bag

To spark your imagination. A jewellery assortment of earrings, choker and pendant. Vary designs as you please

jewellery

By crocheting silver or gold lamé thread over plastic curtain rings, then sewing them together, you can fashion a choker, earrings, or pendant. To vary, try out different combinations. Belts can also be made in this manner and can be fastened with a bead closing.

Materials: 2-ply silver or gold lamé thread, 70 metre (75 yd) spool. 5.00 steel crochet hook. Curtain rings: 2 cms ($\frac{5}{8}$") for choker, earrings; 2 cms, 2.5 cms, 3 cms ($\frac{5}{8}$", $\frac{7}{8}$", $1\frac{1}{8}$") for pendant.

CHOKER: Knot thread around ring, ch 1, work 31 dc in ring, join with sl st. For next round, * ch 4, sk 2 sts, dc in next st, rep from * around. Join with sl st. Fasten off. Make 11 rings or amount to fit around neck. Place rings side by side and sew meeting loops together. For ties, attach thread to a lp of each end ring, ch 50, dc in 2nd ch from hook and in each ch to end. To add beads, sew one to the centre of each ring and between each ring.

EARRINGS: Make 4 rings as above and sew 2 together for each earring. Attach beads and ear fastenings.

PENDANT: Work 1 htr rnd in each ring until filled. Sew rings in design shown or in your own design. To make pendant chain, attach thread to top ring on one side, ch 1. Work 3 dc, ch 1, turn. Continue 3 dc rows until chain measures 33 cms (13") or desired length. Fasten off. Sew to top ring on other side. Ring design can also be sewn to belts or collars.

Lace trim. A succession of floral motifs joined while being made

lace trim

FIRST MOTIF: Crochet cotton in various colours or the same colour. 5.00 steel hook. Ch 5, join with sl st to form ring.

Rnd 1: In ring work (dc, ch 4, dble tr, ch 4)6×, join to first dc. Fasten off.

Rnd 2: Attach wool to any dble tr, dc in same place, * ch 6, dc in 4th ch from hook, ch 2 (picot = pc made), dc in next dble tr, rep from *, end ch 6, dc in 4th ch from hook, ch 2, join to first dc.

Rnd 3: In join work (dc, ch 3, dc), * ch 9, sk pc, (dc, ch 3, dc) in next dc, rep from *, end ch 9, sk pc, join to first dc. Fasten off.

Rep rnds 1 and 2 for as many motifs as you wish. Attach motifs as follows: (rnd 3 for 2nd motif) in join work (dc, ch 3, dc), ch 4. Dc in lp of first motif. (2nd motif) ch 4, sk pc, (dc, ch 3, dc) in next dc, ch 4. Dc in next lp on first motif. (2nd motif) ch 4, sk pc, (dc, ch 3, dc) in next dc, continue from row 3 rep. Fasten off. Attach next motif; 2nd motif will now become first motif and so on.

crocheting with beads

It is possible to add an occasional bead or a bead design to any of the motifs or patterns that have been given. The process, a simple one, is as follows: String the required number of beads onto the thread that will be used. Push beads down out of the way, make starting chain and crochet as usual. Whenever a bead is to be used, push it up to the hook, hold in front of work and make the next stitch around it. Then continue as usual.

window hanging

For a creative approach to the use of motifs try a geometric design. The window hanging illustrated here is made with pearl cotton and is based on the repetition of seven motifs. The motifs are made separately, then joined and attached to a crocheted hoop.

Materials: Crochet cotton, seven 45 metre (50 yd) balls. 5.00 steel crochet hook. 28 cm (11″) lampshade ring (open centre).

PATTERN STITCH: Motif with clusters and picots.

TO MAKE ONE MOTIF, 9 cms (3½″): Ch 6, join with sl st to form ring.

Rnd 1: Ch 3 (counts as first st), work 11 tr in ring, join with sl st to top of ch-3.

Rnd 2: Ch 4 (counts as 1 tr and 1 ch), * tr in next st, ch 1, rep from * around, join to 3rd ch of ch-4 (12 tr with ch 1 between).

Rnd 3: Ch 3, (wrh, insert hook in join, pull up a lp)4× (9 lps), wrh and through 8 lps on hook, wrh and through 2 lps on hook (4 tr cl made), ch 3, * (wrh, insert hook into next st, pull up a lp)5× (11 lps), wrh and through 10 lps on hook, wrh and through 2 lps on hook (cl), ch 3, rep from * around. Join to first cl.

Rnd 4: Ch 3, 4 tr in ch-3 sp of pr r, * tr in next cl, 4 tr in next ch-3 sp, rep from * around (60 tr). Join to top of ch-3.

Rnd 5: * Dc between next 2 sts (over cl), ch 6, sk 5 sts, rep from * around. Join to first st.

Rnd 6: * In ch-6 sp work (4 dc, ch 4, dc in 4th ch from hook [picot], 4 dc), rep from * around. Join to first st.

Fasten off. Rep for 6 more motifs. Do a row of dc around ring. Join round and make a 46 cm (18″) chain for hanging.

Block each motif; place 6 in a circle with the 7th in centre. Sew together by joining two picots of each motif. Sew joined motifs to ring.

(Above) Window hanging of seven motifs. Considered a good luck charm in Sweden. Joined motifs are attached to crochet-covered hoop. (Below) Detail of one motif shows joining of picots

'Owl', wall hanging, 24 cms × 41 cms (9½" × 16"), worked in double crochet throughout

wall hanging 24 cms × 41 cms (9½" × 16")

Inspired by an African wooden mask depicting an owl, this wall hanging uses double knitting wool and is in double crochet throughout. The use of this stitch provides a closely worked, neutral background upon which a three-colour design can be effectively seen. The wall hanging is small and its purpose is to introduce you to the possibilities of creative design in crochet.

Materials: Double knitting wool, 50 gm (2 oz) balls, 1 ball each: black, rust, 2 balls white.
3.50 crochet hook. Bobbins.

Gauge: 5 sts = 2.5 cms (1").

Note: If wool has to be carried across more than 3 sts, attach new bobbin. Always carry wool loosely across wrong side of work.

Ch 46 with black. (The piece is crocheted from top to bottom.)

Row 1: Dc in 2nd ch from hook and in each ch across. Attach rust and ch 1. Turn.

Row 2: With rust dc in first st working last wrh and pulling through with black (colour changes are made by pulling new colour through with last wrh). With black, dc in each of next 2 sts, attach white, dc in each of next 2 sts, carrying black loosely across back of work dc in each of next 2 sts with black, carrying white across back dc in each of next 2 sts with white. Attach black, dc in each of next 25 sts, attach white, dc in each of next 2 sts, attach black, dc in each of next 2 sts, carrying white across back dc in each of next 2 sts with white, carrying black across back dc in each of next 2 sts with black, attach rust, dc in each of next 2 sts, ch 1 with black, turn.

Rows 3–78: Continue working dc, following colour changes on graph.

TO MAKE EYES: Directions below are for one eye; rep for other. With white ch 6, join with sl st to form ring.

Rnd 1: Ch 1, work 10 dc in ring. Attach black, join with sl st.

Rnd 2: With black ch 1, 2 dc in first st, * dc in next st, 2 dc in next st, rep from * around, join to first st with rust.

Rnd 3: With rust ch 1, dc in first st, 2 dc in next st, * dc in each of next 2 sts, 2 dc in next st, rep from * around. Join to first st with black.

Rnd 4: With black ch 1, * 2 dc in next st, dc in each of next 3 sts, join to first st with white.

Rnd 5: With white, sl st in each st around. Fasten off.

To finish, block, sew eyes in place. Make a 4-strand, 15 cm (6") fringe as indicated on graph.

GRAPH FOR WALL HANGING

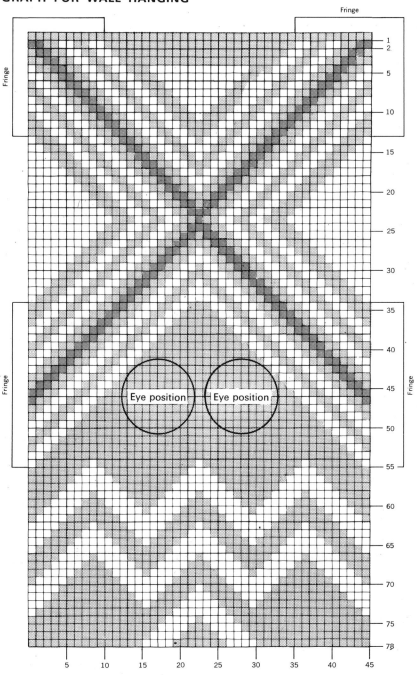

Detail of wall hanging showing colour changes worked in double crochet

Hairpin Lace Crochet

With a hairpin loom you can crochet lace strips to use as decorative edging, to insert between areas of solid crochet, or to join for items such as placemats, stoles, tablecloths, or bedspreads. Looms come in several shapes and adjust to various widths.

Hairpin lace placemat of crochet cotton. 43 cms × 30 cms (17½″ × 12″)

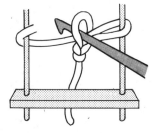

Starting of lace strip. One chain stitch made

3 STEPS IN MAKING LACE STRIP

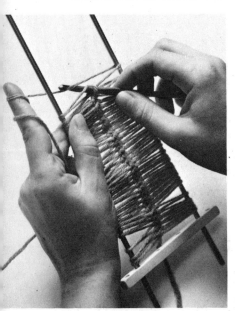

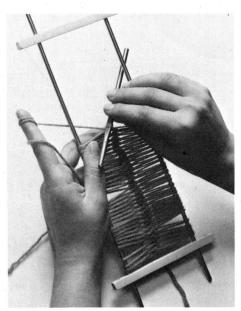

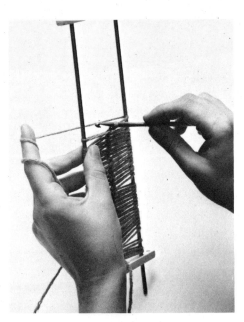

1. Double crochet being made

2. Turn hook end down, other end behind prong. Turn loom right to left towards you

3. Bring hook into crochet position. Work a dc. Note that loops are pushed down while working

TO MAKE A LACE STRIP:

1. Begin with a slip knot as usual. Hold loom in left hand; hold hook between prongs. Wrap thread front to back around right-hand prong, wrh, and pull through 1 ch (diag., facing page).

2. Turn hook as shown (centre photo). Turn loom from right to left towards you (thread will automatically wind around right-hand prong). Bring hook into crochet position, work 1 dc under top left lp.

Rep step 2 throughout. Push lps down as you work. When loom becomes crowded, remove bottom bar and slip off all but 4 lps. Replace bar. If a lot of lps are being made, keep count by marking every 25th one on each side. For easier joining, twist lps when inserting hook.

lace placemat 43 cms × 30 cms (17½″ × 12″)

Materials: Crochet cotton, 25 gm (1 oz).

             2.50 steel crochet hook. Hairpin loom set at 3.75 cms (1½″) width.

Gauge: 5 lps = 2.5 cms (1″).

Working 2 dc into each left-hand lp make 6 strips, each one with 75 lps on each side. Join by placing strips side by side. Attach thread at top or bottom, ch 1, insert hook *back* to *front* (this twists st) through first 3 lps on right-hand strip, dc, ch 3, insert hook *front* to *back* through first 3 lps on left-hand strip, dc, * ch 3, insert *back* to *front* through next 3 lps on right, dc, ch 3, insert *front* to *back* through next 3 lps on left, dc, rep * to end. Fasten off. Attach next strip.

To finish short edge, attach thread to one side, and, keeping work flat, do 1 row dc along edge, turn, sl st in each st across. Fasten off and do other edge. Block.

Other ways to join lace strips are described below and are shown to the right. You can also join with a favourite pattern stitch.

A. (top) Attach thread, work dc in each lp of each strip, ch 1, turn, dc in dc. Fasten off. Join strips by weaving through dc rows.

B. (centre) Attach thread, pick up 3 lps of right strip, dc, (pick up next lp of left strip and dc)3×, * pick up 6 lps of right strip, dc, (pick up next lp of left strip and dc)6×, rep from *, end (pick up lp of left strip and dc)3×, pick up 3 lps of right strip, and dc.

C. (bottom) With hook pick up first 3 lps of left strip, then first 3 lps of right strip, pull right strip lps through left strip lps on hook. Pick up next 3 lps of left strip and pull through right strip lps on hook. Continue in this fashion. At end thread a needle with matching thread and sew remaining 3 lps flat for a smooth edge.

METHODS OF JOINING STRIPS

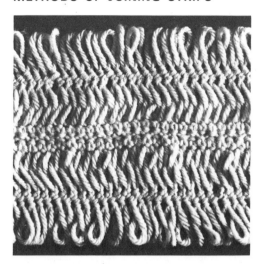

A. Strips joined with double crochet for a flat look

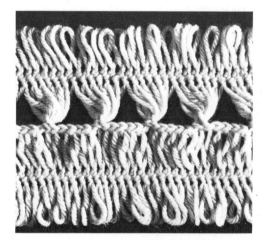

B. Contrasting edges — one gathered, the other straight

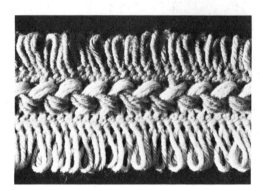

C. Braided effect worked by pulling loops through in groups

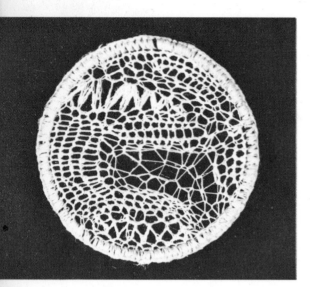

Crocheted wall piece, 20.5 cms (8")
diameter, worked in linen. 1967

Multiple of Stitches

For definition and purpose, see page 26. Pattern stitches and projects
are listed in the order they appear in the book.

Shell st	6+4	Yellow Stole	Uneven no.
Filet mesh	Uneven no.	Placemat Pattern No. 1	13+4
Open shell	6+4	Placemat Pattern No. 2	7+2
Cluster st	3+1	Placemat Pattern No. 4	20+10
Puff st	4+3	Curtain	22+10
Popcorn st	4+3	Baby's Blanket	6+1
Crossed treble crochet	Even no.	Striped Rug	Even no.
Solomon's knot	5+1	Clutch Handbag	Uneven no.
Lanyard Tote Bag	3+1	White Shoulder Bag	2+4
Pink Stole	4+1	Ski Band	Uneven no.
Mohair Shawl	Uneven no.	Tri-colour Hat	Even no.
		Variegated Scarf	Even no.

Suppliers

CROCHET WOOLS, YARNS AND HOOKS

General Enquiries

Leisurecraft Centre,
Search Press Ltd,
2–10 Jerdan Place,
London, SW6 5PT

Mrs Mary Allen,
Turnditch, Derbyshire

E. J. Arnold and Son Limited,
(School Suppliers),
Butterley Street,
Leeds, LS10 1AX

Art Needlework Industries Ltd,
7 St Michael's Mansions,
Ship Street,
Oxford, OX1 3DG

The Campden Needlecraft
Centre,
High Street,
Chipping Campden,
Gloucestershire

Craftsman's Mark Ltd,
Broadlands, Shortheath,
Farnham, Surrey

Fresew,
97 The Paddocks,
Stevenage,
Herts, SG2 9UQ

Harrods Ltd,
London, SW1

Thomas Hunter Ltd,
16 Saville Row,
Newcastle-upon-Tyne,
NE1 8GS

Mace and Nairn (cottons only),
89 Crane Street,
Salisbury, Wiltshire

The Needlewoman Shop,
146–8 Regent Street,
London, W1R 6BA

Nottingham Handcraft Company,
(School Suppliers),
Melton Road,
West Bridgford,
Nottingham, NG2 6HD

Christine Riley (cottons only),
53 Barclay Street,
Stonehaven, Kincardineshire,
AB3 2AR

The Silver Thimble,
33 Gay Street,
Bath

J. Henry Smith Ltd,
Park Road, Calverton,
Woodborough,
nr Nottingham

Suppliers of chenille, carpet warp, uncut rug wool, etc:
J. HYSLOP BATHGATE and Co,
GALASHIELS
SCOTLAND   *(Mail Order)*